FASCINATORS

25 Stylish Accessories to Top Off Your Look

HANNAH SCHEIDIG

RUNNING PRESS
PHILADELPHIA · LONDON

Books published by Running Press are available at special discounts for bulk purchases in the United States by corporations, institutions, and other organizations. For more information, please contact the Special Markets Department at the Perseus Books Group, 2300 Chestnut Street, Suite 200, Philadelphia, PA 19103, or call (800) 810-4145, ext. 5000, or e-mail special.markets@perseusbooks.com.

ISBN 978-0-7624-5967-4
Library of Congress Control Number: 2015954456

E-book ISBN 978-0-7624-5968-1

9   8   7   6   5   4   3   2   1
Digit on the right indicates the number of this printing

Designed by Ashley Haag
Edited by Kristen Green Wiewora
Typography: Futura, Bauer Bodoni, and Adobe Caslon

Running Press Book Publishers
2300 Chestnut Street
Philadelphia, PA 19103-4371

Visit us on the web!
www.runningpress.com

For my wonderful husband Daniel
whose endless love, support, encouragement
and smiles make all of this possible.
Also for my beautiful children and the
rest of my family and friends,
especially my mum and grandma who
inspired me to sew and create.

CONTENTS

Introduction   7

CHAPTER 1: MATERIALS, TOOLS, AND TECHNIQUES

Materials and Tools   13

Making Sinamay Bias Strips   21

Making a Sinamay Base   25

Rolling Sinamay Edge   33

Curling Feathers   36

Burning Feathers   40

Making Fabric Flowers   44

CHAPTER 2: THE PROJECTS

The Mariella   54

The Zara   60

The Naomi   65

The Amanda   71

The Lia   75

The Ottilie   80

The Bethany   86

The Tia   93

The Amelia   99

The Thea   106

The Eloise   112

The Jasmine   117

The Sadie   124

The Emily   131

The Cara   137

The Summer   145

The Mia   150

The Olivia   156

The Isla   163

The Isabella   171

The Anna   178

The Vivienne   186

The Carly   192

The Milly   198

The Lola   204

Templates   212

Acknowledgments   218

Credits   219

Index   220

INTRODUCTION

I have had a long-term love affair with hats and fascinators—
the "fascinating" ladies' headpieces that fall somewhere between a simple
hair clip and traditional, large-brimmed hat. My love of hats goes back
a long way, and my parents' photo albums are full of pictures of little
me with hats or just flowers, stolen from the garden, rammed into my
hair. There's something very striking about fascinators: sitting somewhere
between practical accessories and works of art. I love that an entire outfit
can be perfectly finished off by even the simplest of them.

I decided to turn this passion into a job, and now I have one
of the most enjoyable jobs imaginable: designing and making hats
and fascinators and teaching others to do the same. Back in 2010,
I established my first business, Arabella Bridal (www.arabellabridal.
com), a bridal millinery and accessories online store, focusing on vin-
tage-style fascinators. After numerous phone calls and emails from
customers asking if I offered classes on how to make fascinators, I
decided to give it a go. Several years and hundreds of classes later, the
popularity of our "Made By" craft parties (www.madebycraftparties.
com) has blown me away. There are now hundreds of ladies learning
how to make fascinators every month! More recently I have set up
a website for my non-bridal hats (www.hannahsmillinery.com) due
to the demand from non-bridal customers for hats and fascinators
too. So it's fair to say that making headpieces has now, well and truly,
taken over my life!

At nearly every fascinator-making class I have taught over the past few years, there have been a few recurring questions and common themes. Firstly, without fail someone will ask why on earth I have chosen to make fascinators for a living after a previous career in law. Secondly, there is always at least one person in the class who begins as a worried-looking "I haven't sewn for twenty years, and this is going to be a disaster" sort and becomes a "that was *brilliant*—I had no idea I would be able to do that, and I *did*, and now I want to

make more!" person with a huge smile on her face. Seeing the satisfaction and delight that people get from designing and hand-making a work of art that they can then proudly wear is a wonderful thing and amply demonstrates why I have chosen to do what I now do!

The popularity of fascinators has increased steadily over the past few years, aided hugely by celebrities who favor fascinators over a more traditional hat, including, most famously, the Duchess of Cambridge Kate Middleton. She frequently wears fascinators rather than hats to events. Celebrities from Sarah Jessica Parker to Kate Winslet to Beyoncé have been spotted on the red carpet wearing fascinators. And fascinators are without a doubt becoming the "it" thing to wear at weddings, for the bride, her wedding party, and even for guests, as demonstrated by the hundreds of successful fascinator makers and milliners

on Etsy. Most of my workshop business is focused on brides, bridesmaids, and their friends making fascinators for the big day, as an activity to do together and as a way to give the wedding party a chic, cohesive look. Hardly a day passes that I don't have an email from a bride or mother of the bride, wanting to purchase a fascinator because they "really can't stand wearing" a veil or a dowdy hat, or from a wedding guest who is looking for something a little bit different.

Hat- and fascinator-making is a surprisingly relaxing, fun, and extremely satisfying hobby and—for the lucky ones among us—job. As an added bonus, it doesn't necessarily have to be expensive. While some fascinators do, of course, use beautiful Swarovski crystals and expensive silks, there are plenty of designs that can be made using a few simple, inexpensive materials. The vast majority of designs don't even require the use of a sewing machine (none of the projects in this book will use a sewing machine). Once you have the basic tools, you will be able to make a huge range of styles. It's a very accessible hobby, one that nearly anyone can take up. The key is to master some basic techniques, which can then be used to make lots of different designs. In this book, you will learn how to make a number of beautiful headpieces at home or with friends, using materials that you can easily find in most craft stores or online. Projects range from small sinamay designs (one of the most popular materials to use as a base), to more structured

creations with beautiful embellishments, to festival-worthy floral crowns and silver wired and beaded tiaras.

The projects will range from simple to more complex so that no matter what level your sewing ability, there will be projects to suit you. For those with little experience, the initial, simple step-by-step projects will allow you to work on and master the techniques and skills required to tackle the more complex projects later in the book. The first chapter will discuss the materials and tools that will be used throughout the book and will cover some basic techniques that you can use in a number of the projects. Twenty-five fabulous fascinator projects follow, starting with easy ones, moving on to intermediate, and later developing into more challenging projects. Also included are floral crowns, silver wire tiaras, and a few cute children's fascinator designs. I end each project with ideas for variations that you can make to that particular fascinator, giving many more options for beautiful accessories.

Once you have attempted the projects in this book, I hope that you will be inspired to go on and make more of your own fascinators, experimenting and creating your own designs. I know that my own inspiration for designs comes from a huge variety of sources: from sculptures to nature, architecture to dreams! While some of my designs are planned in detail before I start, particularly when making a bespoke piece for a customer who has specific ideas, others are more organic and are created as I go. I encourage this among the people I teach: there's a lot to be said for going with your gut feeling when designing a new fascinator, as with any work of art. This is one reason I tend to avoid glue and instead hand sew as much as possible: if a disaster does strike, there is always the option to unpick and start again! Another thing to note is that, in this book, I may not teach certain techniques in a way that a traditional millinery school would, but rather in the way that I have found most successful and easiest for people to grasp while teaching my classes over the past few years.

One of the best things about making fascinators is that in terms of design and style, there is not a right and a wrong. The final design and style is a purely personal choice. Give ten people the same basic instructions and materials, and chances are that they'll end up with ten very different fascinators, and none of them will be wrong. Therefore, use these projects as a guide, but feel free to add your own personality to each piece.

Whether you have a wedding to attend as a bride, wedding guest, mother of the bride, or bridesmaid, or perhaps you have an upcoming day out at the races, a black tie event, a garden party, a bachelorette party, a dinner dance, a ball, or just an evening out, whatever the occasion, a fascinator will complete your outfit and make you feel like a million dollars. I hope you have as much fun making these lovely fascinators as I enjoyed designing and creating them!

Chapter 1

MATERIALS, TOOLS, and TECHNIQUES

In this chapter I will describe a few of the most commonly used materials and tools in fascinator-making. I will then go on to describe some basic techniques that shall come in handy in several of the projects in the book.

Materials and Tools

SINAMAY. Sinamay is one of the most widely used materials in the millinery world. It is produced from the fiber of the abaca tree—a banana tree native to the Philippines. It is strong, durable, flexible, and easily dyed. You can buy it in various colors or dye it yourself. It usually comes slightly pre-stiffened.

CRIN OR HORSEHAIR. This is a finely woven, synthetic braiding. Most countries call this crin except in the United States, where it is sometimes still referred to as horsehair, even though it is no longer actually made from horsehair. It comes in a range of widths, from ½ inch (1.3 cm) to 6 inches (15 cm), and a huge range of colors. It can be purchased plain, pleated, or patterned with chenille dots or zigzags. It usually comes with a cotton thread running down one side, which can be used for gathering the braid into nice designs.

VEILING OR NETTING. This is most commonly recognized as the material used to make the popular birdcage veil. Veiling comes in various forms and styles, ranging from French to Russian, plain to spotted, most commonly having a diamond pattern made with varying weights of thread. It can be bought in many colors.

LACE. Lace is a fine, open fabric made from looped, twisted, or knitted cotton or silk, which comes in different patterns and is commonly used for trimming garments. It can be purchased in most haberdashery stores.

FABRIC. There are hundreds of types of fabric, but in these projects I most commonly use silk, satin, taffeta, tulle, tweed, and wool. Silk is a natural fiber produced by silkworms and collected to make fine thread and fabric. Satin is a smooth, glossy fabric produced by a particular weaving technique that produces a shiny surface and a dull back. I also love to work with taffeta and tulle. Taffeta is a crisp, smooth, plain-woven fabric made from silk. Tulle is a netting made from silk, nylon, or rayon—most commonly known for making traditional bridal veils and ballet tutus. You can purchase soft or stiff tulle, depending on what you are using it for and the finish you want to achieve. For a very different look I love to use tweed and wool fabrics. I am lucky enough to live in Scotland and have access to the Isle of Harris, where I can purchase Harris Tweed, which is used in many of my designs. Harris Tweed is a cloth handwoven on the Isle of Harris, in the Outer Hebrides, and is made from pure virgin wool dyed and spun on the island. For those without access to such exceptional tweed, wool-based fabrics give a similar effect. I love working with thicker fabrics due to the lovely structure and warmth they bring to a hat or fascinator. All of these fabrics can be purchased in haberdashery and fabric stores.

PETERSHAM RIBBON AND GROSGRAIN RIBBON. These are strong, flexible corded ribbons usually made from cotton, rayon, viscose, or a blend of fibers and used as trimming or edging. Grosgrain ribbon has a sealed edge, and Petersham has a scalloped edge that is woven into the ribbon, meaning it can curve more easily than Grosgrain.

FEATHERS. There are hundreds of types of feathers from different birds that come in different shapes, sizes, and colors. For each project, I will specify and talk about the kind I use for that particular design.

BEADS. Beads can be purchased in various colors, shapes, and sizes. This includes real and faux pearls, glass beads, plastic beads, and Swarovski crystals.

STIFFENER. Fabric stiffener is used, as its name suggests, to stiffen fabric. You can often use PVA glue mixed with water to achieve the same effect. You can also purchase sinamay stiffener to stiffen sinamay and produce more structure to a design. You can buy sinamay stiffener from many online millinery supply stores.

HAT BLOCK. A hat block is a block carved into the shape of a hat and used to form the initial base shape of a hat or fascinator. Traditionally it is made of wood. Wooden blocks can be expensive to buy, but you can use other wooden or Styrofoam items of the correct shape instead of a traditional block to produce some lovely shapes.

HAIR/HEADBANDS. These are usually made from plastic or metal and are sometimes covered in fabric or wrapped in ribbon, depending on the design. Whether you use plastic, metal, or ribbon-wrapped is really just personal preference. In each project I specify what I have used, but this can be swapped, depending on your preference.

COMBS. Plastic or metal combs are one way of attaching a fascinator to your hair. Whether you use plastic or metal is just personal preference.

HAT ELASTIC. Another way of attaching a fascinator to your hair, hat elastics are hidden in the hair at the back of the head.

BARRETTES/CROCODILE HAIR CLIPS. This is another option for fixing the fascinator to your hair—good for those who are wearing their hair down and who don't want a hair band or hat elastic. I tend not to use these very much, but again that is just personal preference.

WIRE. Various types of wire are used in millinery, including millinery wire, spring wire, florist wire, and craft wire. Millinery wire is very flexible and holds its shape well once it is bent. Spring wire is less flexible so it is better for holding larger shapes. Craft wire tends to be thicker than millinery wire and is often used for making mounts. Florist wire is used to make floral garlands and comes in different thicknesses.

MANNEQUIN HEAD. Mannequin heads are not necessary, but they are useful for displaying your fascinator without having to take it on and off your own head every time you want to see how the overall design is going to sit. Styrofoam mannequin heads can be purchased cheaply online or in craft stores. You'll see that they can also be used when making sinamay bases—for molding the shape of the base in the absence of a hat block.

FABRI-TAC GLUE OR HOT GLUE GUN. While I don't encourage people to use glue too often and instead hand sew as much as possible, as I think it looks much more professional, sometimes glue does come in handy for particularly tricky little bits or if you are simply running out of time. I like Fabri-Tac glue best, as I find it less messy, but if you already have a hot glue gun at home, feel free to use that and be sure not to use too much.

SILK OR FABRIC FLOWERS. These can be made from various materials—silk is one of the most widely used fabrics for making quality faux flowers. You can buy them premade from many online craft suppliers—Etsy has some great ones—or make them yourself (see page 44).

FLOWER-MAKING TOOL KIT. Flower-making tools are a luxury if you decide that you are going to be making a lot of your own flowers. As I describe on page 44, fabric flowers can be made without purchasing expensive flower-making tools, instead using simple metal spoons and a heat source (a gas stove, for example). If, however, you are going to be making a lot of silk flowers, it may be worth investing in flower-making tools. A flower-making tool kit tends to incorporate stainless steel or brass ball tools in various sizes, a hotplate or heating pad to heat them (unless they are electric tools, in which case they will self-heat), a sponge or piece of foam, a dish towel or piece of cotton, silk dye or paint, scissors, glue, florist wire, cotton wool balls, and heat-protective gloves.

BASIC SEWING TOOLS. Range of needles, threads, measuring tape, scissors, iron. You can purchase "milliners needles" (sometimes referred to as "straw needles"), but I tend to just keep a pack of general-use needles handy, with an assortment of sizes ranging from size 3 to 10.

The larger, stronger needles are better for working with stiffer materials such as sinamay, while finer needles are required for things like beading and any fine, decorative stitching. I tend to use Gutermann Sew-All Thread for most of my projects, but any similar thread will be fine.

Techniques

Below are several techniques that are useful to learn, as they are used frequently in fascinator-making and are used in a number of projects in this book. I will often refer back to certain techniques set out below to prevent repeating them each time they are used. Here we will start with some basic stitches.

Throughout the book I will refer to a number of different kinds of stitches: here are the ones most commonly used. For clarity, in the photos I have used embroidery thread and felt in contrasting colors, as it is often difficult to see stitches on sinamay.

RUNNING STITCH OR STRAIGHT STITCH. To do this, bring your needle up through the fabric or sinamay from the backside (wrong side) and pull the thread until the knot catches on the backside. Next make a short stitch. Then, continuing in the same direction, bring the needle and thread down, back up, and repeat. Try to keep your stitch length as even as possible. When you come to the end, simply secure the thread with a small stitch on the wrong side of the fabric.

STAB STITCH. This is an important millinery stitch, as the result is an almost invisible stitch on the backside of the fabric or sinamay—important when sewing an area of the fascinator that is going to be on show when being worn.

To make a stab stitch, bring the needle and thread up from underneath, and go back down very close to where you came up—if sewing on sinamay, the stitches on the front side should ideally catch just one weave whereas the stitches on the back can

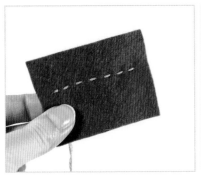

BLANKET STITCH

be up to ½ inch (1.3 cm) apart. If sewing on sinamay, once you have caught one weave and put the needle back down through, make sure it goes down at an angle so that you don't go through the same hole. I use this stitch a lot, as I often don't want my stitches to show. Here you can see the stitches from the front and back.

BLANKET STITCH. The blanket stitch can be used for various things, but in this book you will be using it mainly to secure the wire to the edge of sinamay.

Step 1. To do a blanket stitch, bring your needle and thread from the backside to the front side until the knot catches on the reverse side of the fabric, ¼ inch (0.6 cm) from the edge of the fabric. Put the needle back through the fabric (but don't push it all the way through the fabric) a small distance away (⅛ inch/3 mm) from where it came out, with the needle pointing upward so that the point of the needle can be seen poking up over the edge of the fabric. Take the thread in your fingers at the point where it came through to the front of the fabric and loop it around the point of the needle that is protruding out the back of the fabric. Now pull the needle all the way through the fabric so that it runs along the edge of the fabric.

Step 2. Now insert the needle ½ inch (1.3 cm) along the fabric in the direction you are sewing, again about ¼ inch (6 mm) from the edge, so that the needle is once again pointing upward and is visible from the front. Wrap the thread around the point of the needle and pull the needle through so that the thread now runs along the edge of the fabric and then downward.

Repeat Step 2 along the edge of the fabric as far as required. When you come to the end, simply secure the thread with a small stitch on the backside of the fabric.

TECHNIQUE
1

Making Sinamay Bias Strips

Sinamay bias strips are used in many designs of fascinators. While you can purchase premade strips, they can be fairly expensive, and you will be limited in color and width. Bias strip is really easy to make from sinamay fabric, using a color that matches the rest of your design and your outfit, in any width and length that you like.

MATERIALS

Sinamay sheet: You will need the diagonal measurement of the sinamay to be however long you would like your bias strip to be, so if you want to make a 1-yard strip (91.5 cm), you will need a sinamay square of approximately 25½ x 25½ inches (65 cm x 65 cm)

Tape measure

Fabric scissors

Iron

1. Lay out your sinamay sheet. Take one corner and fold it across to the opposite edge, creating a large triangular shape. Push along the crease, down the long edge of the triangle.

2. Open up the triangle and cut along the crease. This is called cutting on the bias. (The bias is the diagonal part of a woven fabric: it has more stretch).

3. Decide how wide you want your bias strip to be. In this example I want the resulting bias strip to be ¾ inch (2 cm) wide. You need to start with a width four times wider than the end product, so I measure 3 inches (7.5 cm) from the edge, then fold all the way down. Cut along this fold to create a 3-inch (7.5 cm) strip of sinamay that is cut on the bias.

4. Fold this strip in half lengthwise and press down using your fingers, then iron along the crease using a cooler setting. (Note: a hot iron will burn and/or stretch the sinamay.)

5. Open the folded strip back up again, then fold in each edge toward the centerline created by the fold. Leave a small gap (about ⅛ inch/3 mm) in the center. Now fold both of the two folded halves together again using the original center crease. You will now have a strip that is four layers thick. This can then be ironed a final time to hold it in place.

6. Optional. If you would like your strip to be longer and thinner, the finished bias strip can simply be stretched using your hands and/or the iron. This is when the small gap you left (at Step 5) will come into play: it allows the strip to be stretched and narrowed without any sharp, raw edges overlapping and poking out.

7. When you are satisfied with the width and length, cut off any untidy ends. You have a completed strip of sinamay bias that can be used to edge your sinamay bases or be twisted into fabulous shapes as part of your fascinator design.

Making a Sinamay Base

Many fascinators are designed with a sinamay base as the underlying base layer onto which you can build and embellish your desired design. Many hats and fascinator bases are traditionally made using sinamay, millinery wire, a hat block, and millinery stiffener.

Here I show you a simple technique to make a basic round sinamay hat base. This technique can be adapted to make larger or other shaped bases, so I then explain how to adapt it to make a pillbox hat base, which you will use in project 13. We'll use this technique several times throughout the book, so it's a good one to master.

Simple Sinamay Base

MATERIALS

Sinamay fabric (how much you need will depend on the size of the fascinator base that you want to make: here I am making a 4 inch/10 cm base)

Millinery wire

Wire cutters

A template to draw around (try cups, saucers, plates, or bowls)

Floral tape or masking tape

Sinamay bias strip or Petersham ribbon (page 21) (you need enough to go around the circumference of your template plus an extra 1 inch/2.5 cm)

Fabric scissors

A hat block, Styrofoam mannequin head, or other wooden item of the right shape

Plastic wrap

Sinamay stiffener

A small household sponge

Glass head pins or blocking pins. You can use other pins as long as they have three characteristics: firstly, they must be hard so that they don't bend—preferably steel pins; secondly, and this is very important, they must not rust, as you will be applying water and stiffener; thirdly, they should not be so thick that they leave big holes in your hat block (such as pins that are meant for use with cork boards). If they do, your hat block will be ruined very quickly.

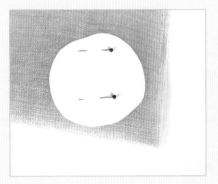

1. Draw and cut out a 4-inch-diameter (10 cm) template on a piece of paper. Fold over the sinamay sheet so that it is double thickness. Pin the paper template onto the double-thickness sinamay and cut around the template to have two identical circles of sinamay.

2. Measure out a length of millinery wire to fit round the circumference of the circle, plus about 1 inch (2.5 cm) that will be used to connect the ends. Overlap the ends by ½ inch (1.3 cm) and double check that the wire ring is the correct size and sits on the edge of the sinamay circles.

3. Once it is the correct size, bind the ends together using the floral or masking tape.

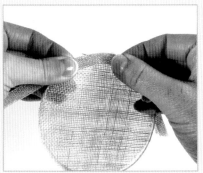

4. The wire then has to be secured to the edge of the double sinamay circle using a blanket stitch (see page 19 at the end of the Technique section on how to do this). Try to make your stitches about ½ inch (1.3 cm) apart and about ¼ inch (6 mm) in from the edge of the sinamay (this is to prevent the edge of the sinamay circle from fraying).

5. Cover the wire edge using either sinamay bias strip or Petersham ribbon. You can choose a matching or complementary color for this, depending on your intended design. If using Petersham ribbon, simply fold this over the edge of the base and sew it in place using stab stitches every ⅕ inch (5 mm) (see how to do this type of stitch on page 18). For sinamay bias strip, take your bias strip and trim off any frayed ends diagonally. Open up the bias strip and place it over the edge of the wired sinamay circles. Secure the bias around the edge with a stab stitch, starting to sew about ½ inch (1.3 cm) from the end of the bias strip.

6. When you have sewn nearly all the way around, tuck the end of the bias strip under the other end and sew neatly in place.

If you want a flat shape, jump to Step 9 below. This will result in a flat, circular fascinator base. However, you can create a curved base that will follow the curve of your head by following Steps 7 and 8 before moving on to Step 9.

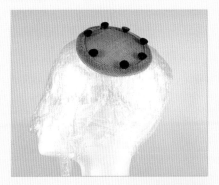

7. Take your mannequin head and cover it in plastic wrap, or alternatively use a rounded wooden object of the right shape, or of course a hat block, if you have one, covered in plastic wrap. Soak the fascinator base in water. You can either put it under hot tap water (being very careful not to burn yourself) or place it in a bowl of hot water for a few seconds. Place the wet fascinator base on the mannequin head and use the glass head pins (or blocking pins) to secure it all the way around the edge.

8. Follow the package instructions on the fabric stiffener (some will already be diluted, and some may require dilution with water before using), then dab some stiffener all over the fascinator base using a sponge. Leave it to dry.

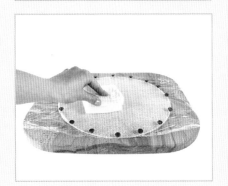

9. If you want a flat shape, pin this circle to a flat board such as a wooden chopping board covered in plastic wrap, using pins to hold it in place, then follow the package instructions on the fabric stiffener and dab some stiffener all over the fascinator base using a sponge. Leave it to dry.

This basic technique can be adapted to create different shapes of sinamay hat bases. For project 13 (page 124) we use a pillbox hat base, and for project 15 (page 137) we use a biscuit-shaped hat base, so on the following pages I explain how to adapt the method above to create these shapes.

Hat blocks can be very expensive, and if you're just starting out it's probably better to make your own. For small bases you can use a Styrofoam mannequin head (which can be purchased cheaply online or from craft stores) covered in plastic wrap (this keeps your sinamay from sticking once you have applied the stiffener). For different-shaped bases, you can use various wooden household items—wooden bowls of different shapes and sizes, or even cutting boards for flat shapes. Again, cover them with plastic wrap before pinning on and stiffening your sinamay. Once you get into more complex shapes—very large saucer bases with upturned lips, etc.—you can either make your own blocks from denser Styrofoam (though this is a craft in itself) or you will need to invest in a hat block or two. If you're lucky you can sometimes pick up secondhand hat blocks online.

Pillbox Hat Base

MATERIALS

You will need the same materials as for the simple round base (page 26), except that you won't need the template to draw around and you will need a pillbox hat base or wooden bowl of a similar shape to use in place of the mannequin head. For project 13 we need a 6-inch-diameter (15 cm), 1½-inch-deep (3.8 cm) pillbox hat base.

Your sinamay fabric will need to fit over the whole hat block. I recommend always cutting more than you need to make it easier to pull it over the block, so for a 6 x 1½-inch (15 x 3.8 cm) hat block I use two 15-inch-diameter circles of sinamay fabric.

1. Take your hat block or bowl. You can see here the hat block I used next to a very similar basic wooden bowl that would produce a similar shape. I wrapped it in plastic wrap before blocking the sinamay base.

2. Take your two sinamay circles, spray them with water and iron them together on both sides. This makes it slightly easier to handle when blocking. Spray the sinamay again before pinning it onto the block as you did with the simple round base. Another common technique when producing a 3D shape like this is to steam the sinamay rather than spraying it with water before gently shaping it over the block and pinning it around the edges: you can use the steam from a pressing iron for this.

3. Pull the sinamay gently as you shape it over the block but try not to overstretch the sinamay, as you can pull it out of shape. Once pinned onto the block around the edge and stiffener has been applied, you will have to leave it for several hours or overnight to dry. When it is nearly dry, use a cool iron directly on the sinamay to give a nice finish.

4. Trim off the excess sinamay to form a neat edge and wire the edge using the same technique as for the simple round base.

PILLBOX

BISCUIT

ROUND

5. I then used ½-inch-wide (1.3 cm) Petersham ribbon to edge it rather than sinamay bias, as I find it easier to get a smooth edge, but you can use either.

For project 15 I use a biscuit-shaped sinamay base. This can be done using the same materials and technique as for the pillbox hat base above by simply swapping the hat block or wooden bowl for a biscuit-shaped one (so the edges curve under more than a traditional pillbox shape). I have made a biscuit-shaped base using a 6-inch-diameter (15 cm) "biscuit" circular fascinator block. My block has a hollow underside, which allowed me to curl the inner edge of the sinamay base underneath. Once again I finished this off by sewing on a strip of Petersham ribbon. This tidies up the inside of the base and helps it to sit comfortably on the head.

These techniques will enable you to make a curved, round fascinator base, a pillbox hat base, and a biscuit-shaped base. This same technique can be adapted by using different hat blocks or other wooden objects to create different sizes and shapes. It is an important technique to learn, as you will be creating different bases for a number of projects in this book. If you are short on time, you can purchase premade bases in various sizes and shapes from a number of online craft and millinery supply stores by simply searching for "sinamay fascinator bases."

Rolling Sinamay Edge

Sinamay is a woven, natural fiber. When you purchase it in fabric form, it is usually already dyed and has a stiffener on it. When it is cut with scissors, it can leave quite a rough edge, so this step-by-step guide shows you how to roll the edges of sinamay, which eliminates the rough edge and replaces it with a pretty, soft finish. This can be used to form shapes that can be incorporated into a fascinator design, such as the rolled edge leaf I shall teach you to make below, or larger shapes that can form the main part of a fascinator.

Sinamay sheet (size depends on what shape you want to
create: for this leaf, I cut out a leaf shape approximately
10 x 5 inches/25.5 x 12.5 cm)

Scissors

Warm water

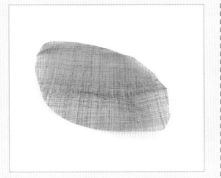

1. Start by cutting the shape you want to form, but add on approximately 1 inch (2.5 cm) all around to allow for the rolled edge. It is best to cut the shape on the bias.

2. Dip the sinamay briefly into warm or hot water—if you leave it in there for more than a couple of seconds it will get too wet, and the edges may begin to break as you roll. The water should not be boiling hot: you should be able to put your hand comfortably into the water. Tuck the edge in and begin to roll the edges tightly back and forth, using your fingers.

3. Because of the glue/stiffener on the sinamay, after rolling this tightly back and forth between your fingers several times, it should hold its shape. Continue this rolling motion all the way around the edge.

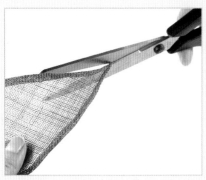

4. You will find that if you are doing a shape that has corners or points, there will be messy ends. All you need to do is twist the two ends together tightly and cut off any excess using scissors.

5. This will leave you with a beautiful rolled-edge leaf shape. This can be used as is or twisted into other shapes, and it can be used as part of the design of a fascinator. Here I simply twisted it in the middle to form two petal-like shapes.

I used this technique to make flowers and longer shapes in projects 2 and 4 (pages 60 and 71).

Curling Feathers

Feathers come in all colors, shapes, and sizes. They make a wonderful embellishment to a fascinator. Curling feathers is a useful technique to learn, as it can really change the look of the feather and often makes it look more interesting. First I will show you how to curl the barbs and vanes of feathers using a goose feather, followed by curling the shaft of the feather using a peacock tail feather. These techniques can be used with many kinds of feathers. You can also use heat to curl larger feathers.

Feathers

Utility knife or sharp scissors

Butter knife

Curling the feather barbs and vanes

1. Take the feather in one hand and the butter knife in the other, with the blunt edge of the butter knife facing the feather.

2. Use your thumb to gently press down small sections of the feather against the blunt edge of the knife and curl them around. Use the same curling technique as you would use to curl ribbon. You may need to repeat this curling motion several times on each section of the feather to obtain a good, tight curl.

3. Carry on with this same technique, using a small section of feather all the way up to the top on both sides of the feather.

Curling the shaft of a feather

1. Take the utility knife or scissors and remove the barbs and vanes down one side of the feather.

2. Now, using the same gentle, pressing motion as you did to curl the barbs of the feathers, gently press the spine of the feather onto the blunt edge of the butter knife and curl it gradually around. Make sure you curl it in the direction of the bare side of the feather, so that the remaining feathers are on the outside of the curl. Do ensure that this is a very gentle, repetitive motion, as otherwise there is a risk of breaking the shaft. When you reach the thinner end of the feather, you can apply a bit more pressure to get a tighter curl at the top.

I used curled feathers in many of my projects: you can see examples in projects 3 and 7 (pages 65 and 86).

Burning Feathers

Burning feathers is a simple technique to learn and gives feathers a very different look by changing their color and texture. It is difficult to get two burnt feathers to look exactly the same due to the fact that they are a natural product, and no two are the same to begin with. If you want multiple burnt feathers to look the same, you may have to burn several.

MATERIALS

Rubber gloves

2 plastic tubs large enough to lay your feathers flat

Chlorine bleach

Water

Old wooden spoon or stick

Feathers for burning

Old dish towel

1. We are using some pheasant tail feathers in this example. This is what they look like before being burnt.

2. Put on your protective rubber gloves. Put some water in one plastic tub, and in the other put just enough bleach to cover the feathers. Put the feathers into the bleach, making sure that they are completely covered by the bleach.

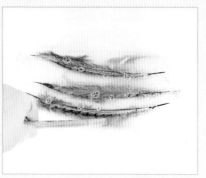

3. Use the end of the wooden spoon to move the feathers around in the bleach to make sure they are completely saturated. Within a minute or so the bleach will start to look a bit cloudy or dirty—some of the color from the feather will run, and some of the barbs of the feather may start to fall off. You'll see little bubbles appear in the bleach as the burning process occurs.

4. When you can see that only the main shaft and some of the barbs remain, move the feathers into the tub of water to clean off the bleach. If you feel that you want them to look more burnt, repeat this process until you have achieved the result you want.

5. Once the feathers have been very well rinsed in the water and you are sure that no bleach remains on them, use your fingers to comb out the feathers and leave them to dry on the dish towel.

6. When the feathers are completely dried out, you can continue to gently comb out the barbs to give them some body. You can then use them as they are or use the curling technique taught on page 36 to curl them.

I use burnt and curled feathers in projects 7 and 15 (pages 86 and 137) and in some of the variations. They look lovely in lots of designs, so this is a useful technique to master.

Making Fabric Flowers

Making fabric flowers is fairly time consuming, but it is a really fun project in itself. If this is your first time making them, it could take you the better part of a day to create one or two. Once you know the techniques involved, you'll be able to make them a bit quicker, and you'll have a lot of fun trying and testing different petal shapes and creating new flowers for your different fascinator projects. Making your own flowers means that you can decide exactly what style, size, and color you want. Any natural fabric will work—you don't have to use silk. Just make sure it's not synthetic, which will melt with the heat. The petal shape depends on the flower you want to make. There are templates on page 212, or you can find templates online by searching for flower petal templates, or in books specifically about fabric or silk flower-making, or you can freehand them using a pen and paper. If you don't have the time or equipment required to make flowers for your projects, there are numerous stores where you can purchase premade silk or other fabric flowers. Etsy, for example, has a great selection of sellers of silk flowers.

MATERIALS

Natural silk fabric (Dupioni, Habotai, or Organza); in this example I used approximately 22 x 13 inches (56 x 33 cm) of Dupioni silk to make a fairly large rose)

Flower-making tools (if you don't have these, you can instead use metal spoons of varying sizes, which you can heat, carefully)

Heat-protective gloves

A block of sponge or foam at least 5 x 5 inches (12.5 x 12.5 cm), covered with a piece of cotton fabric (this is used to shape the flower petals: you can purchase these in craft or haberdashery stores, or use a large dishwashing sponge)

Silk dye or fabric paint

Sharp fabric scissors

PVA glue for stiffening the fabric (or premade fabric stiffener)

Glue (multipurpose or UHU) for sticking petals together

About 16 inches (40.5 cm) of florist or millinery wire per flower

Florist tape

Cotton wool

Everyday craft paintbrushes (one for glue and one if you are dyeing/painting the fabric)

Plastic sheet or something similar to protect your work surface

Tupperware or old plastic container

1 skirt hanger

Templates for rose petals, page 212

1. Lay the fabric on the plastic sheet. Mix 1 part PVA glue with 5 parts water in the plastic Tupperware container to produce a thin, creamy consistency, and paint it onto the fabric using a paintbrush.

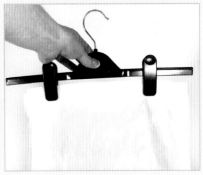

2. Using the skirt hanger, hang this glue-soaked fabric up to dry. It will drip, so make sure you protect the area over which it's hanging.

3. Once this is dry, you now have the option of painting or dyeing the fabric. (If you are using colored fabric and just want to leave it unpainted, jump to Step 5.) Lay your stiffened fabric out on the plastic sheet again and use silk dye or fabric paint to paint the fabric all over. Ensure that you follow the package instructions on the silk dye and fabric paint, as each may have slightly different methods of application. (For example, the silk dye that I used states that once the silk has been painted and is dry, to make the color waterproof the silk needs to be ironed for 5 minutes.)

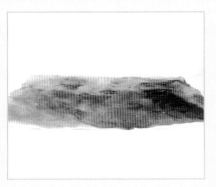

4. If you wish, you can play with the colors and merge them together using water to dilute and blend them on the fabric. Carry on until the fabric is covered (don't worry about reaching the very edges, as these can later be cut off anyway). Once completely painted, leave or hang this to dry as you did in Step 2.

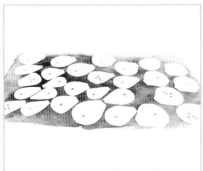

5. Once it is dry, take your petal templates and place them onto the fabric, ensuring that they sit diagonally so that the petals make use of the fabric bias. You can choose to either draw around the petals with a ballpoint pen (pencil tends to smudge) or pin the templates on at the bottom of the petals.

6. Carefully cut out the petal shapes. You will see from the petal templates provided that I used 28 petals in total, so you will need approximately the same number.

7. Before beginning the next step, please ensure that you and the area that you are using are protected from the heat, so that neither you nor the work surface or surroundings are hurt or damaged. Heat up your flower tools, ensuring they are not too hot, otherwise they will burn the fabric. To test the heat, put the hot ball on an old dishcloth or piece of cotton. If it leaves a burn mark, it's too hot and you will need to let it cool down. If you are using a spoon and heating element, heat up the spoon now, again taking lots of care not to burn yourself.

8. Get your cotton-covered sponge block. Holding the base of a petal, push the heated ball (or dome of the spoon) into the petal shape resting on the sponge. Repeat this on all of your petals so that they each form a bowl shape. I've shown both methods so you can see how it might look. Note that I am using a dishcloth to hold the spoon to protect my hands from the heat.

9. Now turn each petal over, and again hold the base. Using the hook tool (or bottom edge of the spoon) press down about ¼ inch (6 mm) from the edge of the petal so that it turns back on itself. Do this all the way around the edge of each petal, leaving the base untouched. Repeat this for all of the petals. You can put away the hot flower tools after this step.

10. The petals should now look like this.

11. Next make the center of your flower. The shape and size of the center will depend on the type of flower you are making. For our rose, we need to form a "bud" center. We can do this using cotton wool and a length of florist wire. Wrap your wire around the center of your piece of cotton wool. Fold the ends of the cotton wool over and wrap the wire around it again, bringing the ends of the wire together and twisting them together, forming a stem. The resulting cotton wool ball should be about 1 inch (2.5 cm) in diameter.

12. Take one of your smallest petals and place some multipurpose glue all over the inside of the petal and stick it onto the cotton wool ball. Repeat this with two more small petals, overlapping the petals so that you cover the cotton wool center completely. This forms the flower base.

13. Add the next three petals by putting glue near the base of the inside of the cups of each petal and sticking them onto the flower base, again making sure that you overlap the petals as you stick them on and making sure the turned-back lips of each petal are facing up and turning outward.

14. Repeat this process of adding glue to the inside base of each cupped petal, and sticking it onto the flower base, each time turning the base and overlapping each petal. You can choose whether you want to see the bud center or have it hidden. If you want it hidden, stick the next petals on slightly higher up the flower, cup the flower in your hand, and use the wire stem to pull firmly downward. For this particular rose, I decided that I wanted to see the bud center, so I stuck all the petals low on the base and just pulled on the wire stem very gently as I formed the flower and stuck the petals on.

15. Once you have stuck on all the petals, leave it to dry for around one hour. You can then tidy up the outer base of the flower by wrapping the base with florist tape.

We're going to use a rose just like this on page 112 in project 11. Try experimenting with different petal shapes and sizes to form different flowers.

Chapter 2

THE PROJECTS

The Mariella

A SIMPLE SINAMAY BIAS LOOP WITH FEATHER EMBELLISHMENT

LEVEL
Easy

APPROXIMATE TIME TO MAKE
1 hour

MATERIALS

43-inch (120 cm) sinamay bias strip (page 21), any width you'd like (¾-inch-width/2 cm bias strip used here)

2 feathers, approximately 5 inches (13 cm) long (I used curled goose feathers: page 36)

Plastic or metal hair comb (I used a 3-inch/7.5 cm comb, as I find it grips the hair well and is small enough to be hidden by the sinamay design, but you can use smaller or bigger ones depending your design and preference.)

Straight pins

Needle and coordinating thread

Scissors

Optional for variations: different feathers, sinamay strips of different widths, beads, round fascinator base, French netting

1. Take the sinamay bias strip and cut it into a 36-inch (91.5 cm) strip and a 7-inch (18 cm) strip. Take your longer piece and form a small loop (using about 8 inches/20.5 cm of the strip) at one end.

2. Now make a second loop of a similar size, forming a figure-8.

3. Repeat this to form a second figure-8 by making a third, slightly larger loop over the top of one side of the figure-8.

4. Form a fourth loop (the same size as the third) over the top of the other side, using the remainder of the bias strip.

5. Pin this shape in place to hold it together. Thread your needle with a double length of thread, for extra strength. Sew through all four of the layers of sinamay at the center point. This may be quite difficult, so try a heavy-duty needle and a thimble if you have trouble.

6. Take your shorter length of sinamay bias strip and form it into a loop, stitching the ends of the loop in place. Then place the loop onto the center point of your double figure-8 and stitch it in place with a few simple stab stitches. (See page 18 for how to do this.)

7. Next you can embellish the piece. Here I have chosen to use two goose feathers that have been curled, but you can use any kind of feathers. Using a mirror, hold the fascinator on your head and move it around until you find a position you're happy with. Then take your feathers and, again using a mirror, move these around until you get those sitting in the direction that you like. The easiest and neatest way to then attach the feathers is to tuck the base of the stems in between the two figure-8 loops and stitch them in place. As the goose feather shafts are quite thick, you should be able to sew through the shaft itself.

8. Now all that is left to do is to attach your comb to the fascinator. Turn the fascinator upside down and lay the comb along the bias strip. Attach the comb with a few stitches between the teeth at either end of the comb.

Variations

You can use the technique of twisting the bias strip into this "double figure-8" to form a number of different fascinators. Try using two different colors or widths of bias strip for the figure-8s, adding veiling underneath the twisted bias strip, using different feathers, sewing the bias strip loops onto a round base, or adding beading in the center of the figure-8s.

The Zara

PROJECT 2

ROLLED-EDGE SINAMAY STRIP DESIGN WITH FEATHER EMBELLISHMENT

LEVEL

Easy

APPROXIMATE TIME TO MAKE

1 hour

MATERIALS

A strip of sinamay cut on the bias, approximately 50 inches (127 cm) long and 3 inches (7.5 cm) wide, tapering to about ½ inch (1.3 cm) wide at each end

Scissors

Straight pins

Needle and coordinating thread

Decorative feathers (I used 2 arrowhead turkey feather quills)

3-inch-wide (7.5 cm) metal or plastic comb

Optional for variations: different widths of sinamay or different types of feathers

1. Using the sinamay edge-rolling technique taught on page 33 (Technique 3), roll the edges of this sinamay strip. Cut any excess ends off to form neat ends to the strip.

2. Twirl this rolled-edge sinamay strip into a shape that you like. I have twisted it over on itself five times in a random formation. Once you have formed a shape that you like, pin it in place.

3. Using a thread color that matches the sinamay, sew this shape in place with small stitches through the central points where the rolled-edge sinamay strip crosses over.

4. Take your feathers and position them where you would like them to sit. Sew these in place. If you are sewing them on, and the feathers have sufficiently thick shafts, you can sew through the actual shaft. With this design, because the stitches that attach the feathers may be visible, it is best to sew through the shaft sideways to avoid seeing your stitches. (Tip: If you find it difficult to get your needle through the shaft, try using a thimble or pushing your needle against a hard surface to get it through to avoid hurting your finger.) Sew the feathers about 3 inches (7.5 cm) up from the bottom of the shaft. If you find the feathers are wobbling, make another stitch about ½ inch (1.3 cm) above that. Use a thread that matches the color of the feather to hide the stitching.

5. Use a mirror to decide which direction you would like the fascinator to sit on your head. Attach the fascinator directly to a comb by sewing in between the teeth at each end of the comb.

Variations

You can vary the color and style of this design by making wider, narrower, shorter, or longer rolled-edge sinamay strips and varying the types of feathers used as embellishments.

The Naomi

FEATHER-EMBELLISHED BASE WITH BROOCH DETAIL

LEVEL
Easy

APPROXIMATE TIME TO MAKE
2 hours

MATERIALS

A selection of approximately 8 to 10 feathers (I used a selection of peacock sword and tail feathers)

Lace or ribbon trimming (I used 13 inches/33 cm of lace)

6-inch (15 cm) round sinamay base (page 25)

Brooches or buttons to embellish

Fabri-Tac glue or a hot glue gun (I prefer Fabri-Tac, but a standard hot glue gun works fine)

Needle and thread

Scissors

3-inch-wide (7.5 cm) metal or plastic comb

Optional for variations: different widths of lace and different types of feathers

1. Attach the comb to the underside of the sinamay base at the side by sewing between a few of the teeth at either side of the comb.

2. Take each of your feathers and decide how long you want them to be and whether you want them curled or not. These peacock sword feathers are each approximately 13 inches (33 cm) long. I curled four of them, using the techniques taught on page 36 and trimmed them to about 9 inches (23 cm) each. I then trimmed the tail feathers to 6 inches (15 cm).

3. Once you have curled and trimmed the feathers, lay them onto the sinamay base and arrange them as you want them to sit. Choose whether you want to glue the feathers, or if you want to sew them on individually. Usually I would sew these on, but gluing them is an easy option. If you are gluing them on, glue about ½ inch (1.3 cm) up from the base of the feathers. This means the glue will be hidden by other embellishments (lace or brooches), but you will need room to sew those embellishments on. (It can be difficult to sew through glue, so try not to glue exactly where you want to sew.)

4. Next take any ribbons or trimmings you want to add. To add lace loops, make a loop using half (6.5 inches/16.5 cm) of your lace, then another of equal size. Stitch the two ends and the folded point together in place at the base of your feathers.

5. Finally, cover the base of the feathers and lace/ribbon trimmings with the brooches or buttons of your choice. Here we have chosen a 1¼-inch-diameter (3.2 cm) button. When you sew it on, ensure that it covers any messy ends of feathers and trimming.

Variations

Use different feathers and trimmings to produce various designs. Also try edging the base with a lace trimming for a different look.

The Amanda

LARGE SHAPED ROSE WITH FRENCH NETTING

LEVEL
Easy

APPROXIMATE TIME TO MAKE
1 to 2 hours

MATERIALS

Sinamay strip 32 inches (81.5 cm) long and 4 to 5 inches (10 to 12.5 cm) wide, tapering in at each end

Straight pins

Needle and thread

Approximately 50 inches (127 cm) French netting (9 inches/23 cm wide)

Small piece of sinamay bias strip (page 21), approximately 1 x 2 inches (2.5 x 5 cm)

Narrow metal or plastic headband

Optional for variations: large fabric flower and/or feathers

1. Roll one long edge of the sinamay strip using the technique taught on page 33. As I wanted a "shabby chic" look for this particular design, I did a looser roll than what is shown on page 34 simply by not rolling the edge as tightly between my fingers.

2. Once you have rolled along the long edge of your shape, twist the rolled-edge sinamay strip into a spiral to form a rose, starting with a tight center and spiraling the sinamay outward. Make sure that the end you started with is tucked inside the middle so that you can't see it. When you get to the other end of the strip, tuck it behind the back of the rose.

3. Hold the gathered point of your rose in one hand. Pin this in place, then sew through all layers of the spiral to secure it.

4. Take the French netting and hold it at the midpoint of the two short ends. Gather it down the centerline until you are holding it in one central point, like a big, puffy bow.

5. Sew the gathered point together, ensuring you catch all the netting to hold it tight.

6. Now attach the netting to the rose, sewing the gathered point just at the back of the main rose design.

7. Put the headband on your head. Use a mirror to position the rose and netting design where you want it to sit on the band, and mark this point on the band using something such as a small piece of masking tape. Next turn the sinamay design upside down, lay the headband in your chosen direction, and position the sinamay bias strip on top of the headband, sandwiching the band between the rose design and the strip, to hold the design on the band. Sew a tight running stitch (see page 18) down either side of the headband, stitching the sinamay bias rectangle onto the back of the sinamay rose design to hold it in place.

Variations

This piece can be varied by making a large fabric flower instead of the sinamay rose, by using different colors of netting, or by adding feathers beneath the flower.

The Lia

ROUND SINAMAY BASE WITH BEADING AND A FABRIC RUFFLE

LEVEL
Easy

APPROXIMATE TIME TO MAKE
2 to 3 hours

MATERIALS

2 x 8-inch (5 x 20.5 cm) rectangle of thick fabric such as wool or tweed

Needle and coordinating thread

4-inch (10 cm) round sinamay base (see page 25)

Approximately 200 small (5 mm) bugle beads

3-inch-wide (7.5 cm) metal or plastic comb

Optional for variations: different beads, a different-shaped base, or more fabric for a larger ruffle

1. Take your rectangle of thick fabric and do a running stitch down the middle of the ruffle, gathering the fabric as you go. Gather it until the ruffle is just less than 4 inches (10 cm) long. Check that it sits on the base toward the side, within the sinamay edging. Once you are happy with the size, secure the ruffle by fastening off your stitching on the underside of the ruffle.

2. Attach the ruffle to the base with a couple of stitches in the center of each end and in the center middle point of the ruffle.

3. Sew on the bugle beads to cover the remainder of the sinamay base, keeping the beads inside the sinamay bias edging of the base. I find that it looks best if you try to sew the beads on in a random arrangement, although I have done one neat row just inside of the sinamay base edge. When sewing them on, always ensure that you start by bringing your needle up from underneath the base so that the knot at the end of the thread is hidden underneath.

4. Before you attach the comb, use a mirror or mannequin head to place the fascinator where you want it to sit and to check the direction in which you're going to attach the comb. Attach the comb by sewing between a few of the teeth at each end.

Tip

Whenever you are beading, do an extra, small stitch on the underside of the base after every tenth bead. This means that if you drop your needle at any point, or your thread breaks, you don't lose all your hard work—only the last ten beads. This can really save your sanity (speaking from experience)!

Variations

This piece can be varied by using different beads or pearls, making the ruffle smaller or larger, or using different kinds of fabric for the ruffle: any thick fabric should work well.

The Ottilie

SINAMAY BOW FASCINATOR WITH BIRDCAGE VEIL

LEVEL
Easy

APPROXIMATE TIME TO MAKE
1½ hours

MATERIALS

1 round sinamay base (I made a 5½-inch/14 cm base) (page 25)

28½ inches (72.5 cm) of 1-inch-wide (2.5 cm) sinamay bias strip (page 21)

Needle and coordinating thread

27 inches (68.5 cm) of 9-inch-wide (23 cm) French netting

3-inch-wide (7.5 cm) metal or plastic comb

Optional for variations: larger base, sinamay fabric for making larger bows, adhesive diamante crystals

1. Cut off 13 inches (33 cm) from the strip of sinamay bias. Form a double loop with this section of sinamay strip.

2. Cut off 12 inches (30.5 cm) and repeat Step 1 to form a second, slightly smaller double loop that shall sit on top of the larger double loop.

3. Put a few stitches through the center of the two loops to hold them in place.

4. Wrap the remaining 3½ inches (9 cm) of sinamay bias around the center of the double bow and secure this with a few stitches underneath.

5. Take your length of French netting, lay it down lengthwise and cut off the top two corners—approximately 4 inches (10 cm) along the edge to create the shape shown in the template on page 213.

6. Using a needle and thread, secure your thread in the bottom corner of the netting (point X in the diagram). Weave the thread in and out of the diamonds of the netting all the way around the edge of the netting, apart from the long, uncut edge—weaving along sides A, B, C, D, and E in the diagram.

7. Once you have woven the thread through all the diamonds, pull it tight. This will gather the netting to form a birdcage veil. Secure this shape with a few stitches through the gathered part of the birdcage veil (points X and Y in the diagram are now pulled together).

8. Take your birdcage veil and attach it to one side of the round base by sewing the gathered point of the birdcage veil to the base with a few stitches. Make sure it sits so that the veil sits over the large part of the base.

9. Next take your sinamay double bow and sit it on top of the gathered part of your birdcage veil.

10. Sew this in place with a few stitches through the center point of the bow.

11. Before you attach the comb, use a mirror or mannequin head to position the fascinator and to check the placement of the comb: make sure it's facing the right direction. Attach the comb by sewing between a few of the teeth at each end of the comb.

Variations

This is a great little project and can be varied in lots of ways: starting with a larger base, making larger or different-shaped bows using sinamay fabric, removing the birdcage veil, or adding some sparkling diamante.

The Bethany

SMALL TEARDROP BASE WITH LACE AND CURLED PHEASANT FEATHER

LEVEL
Intermediate

APPROXIMATE TIME TO MAKE
2 to 3 hours

MATERIALS

Teardrop-shaped fascinator base, approximately 6 x 4½ inches (15 x 11.5 cm) (page 25, forming a teardrop shape instead of a circle)

Lace fabric in a complementary color, cut 1½ inches (3.8 cm) larger than your base all around

8-inch (20.5 cm) strip scalloped-edge lace in the same color as the lace fabric (approximately 2½ inches/6.5 cm wide)

Pheasant feather

Button or brooch

3-inch-wide (7.5 cm) metal or plastic comb

Straight pins

Needle and coordinating thread

Scissors

Optional for variations: felt (the same size as the base), different feathers, different buttons, satin or silk instead of lace fabric

1. If your lace has a "right" and "wrong" side to it, make sure the "right" side is facing downward. Lay your base upside down on top of the lace.

2. Pull the lace over the edges of the base and pin this in place all the way around underneath, pulling it reasonably tightly as you go to ensure that the lace sits neatly on the base when you turn it back over.

3. Once it is all pinned in place, use a simple running stitch with small stitches to sew this in place all the way around. If you sew onto the underside of the sinamay edging of the base, rather than all the way through to the top, your stitches won't show on the top.

4. If you have lots of excess lace underneath, simply trim this off, being careful not to snip any of your stitching. You should now have a neat, lace-covered base.

5. Next take your strip of scalloped-edge lace (you could use the edge of the lace fabric if it has a scalloped edge). Gather the lace into a fan shape with the scalloped edge pointing outward. Sew through the gathered part of the lace fan to hold this shape in place.

6. Sit this fan shape onto the wide end of the teardrop base. Make sure it comes right to the end. Sew this gathered part of the fan to the base in the center of the wide end. If you have untidy edges, leave them hanging over the edge.

7. Wrap untidy edges to the underside of the base, pin them in place, and sew them to the underside (again try to sew onto the base's edging so as not to see the stitching on top of the fascinator) to create a neat finish.

8. Now comes the fun part of choosing how to embellish the lovely lace base. I chose here to use a curled burnt pheasant feather and small button brooch. Insert your chosen feather into the ruffle of lace, and stitch it in place with a few stitches, hiding them among the ruffle.

9. I then sewed on my brooch: this can simply be pinned on if it's a pin brooch.

10. For the perfectionists among you, there is an easy way to hide any messy stitching on the underside of the fascinator before attaching the comb. This process can be used for most fascinators that have a sinamay base. All you need to do is cut a piece of felt in the same shape as the base but about ½ inch (1.3 cm) smaller than the base. Pin the felt in place, and then sew a small running stitch all around the edge of the felt. Once again, try to stitch onto the underside of the sinamay base edging rather than stitching all the way through to the top of the fascinator.

11. Use a mirror to position the fascinator on your head where you would like it to sit. Work out which way the comb needs to be attached to sit in the chosen position, and attach the comb to complete your fascinator.

Variations

To vary this design, try using different types of
feathers and different buttons and brooches, or try
using other fabrics instead of lace.

The Tia

TULLE EXPLOSION WITH OSTRICH QUILL EMBELLISHMENTS

LEVEL
Intermediate

APPROXIMATE TIME TO MAKE
3 to 4 hours

MATERIALS

4-inch (10 cm) round sinamay base (page 25)

3-inch (7.5 cm) strip of sinamay bias at least ½ inch (1.3 cm) wider than your headband

120 inches (305 cm) of 4-inch-wide (10 cm) tulle fabric (this can be in several pieces if you don't have a piece that's long enough)

55 inches (139.5 cm) of 3-inch-wide (7 cm) tulle fabric in a contrasting color

3 ostrich quills, each trimmed to approximately 18 inches (45.5 cm) long

Pressing iron or hair straightener

Straight pins

Headband (mine was covered in ribbon, but you can use any kind of band that you find comfortable)

Needle and coordinating thread

Scissors

Optional for variations: sinamay bias loops and different feathers

1. Put the headband on your head and use a mirror to position the fascinator base on the band where you want the fascinator to sit. Mark the position of the base on the headband using straight pins if it's satin- or ribbon-covered or with tape if it's metal or plastic.

2. Open up the sinamay bias strip and wrap it around the headband where you marked the placement for the fascinator base, pushing it right back up against the long fold. If you're using a metal band, you can glue along the inner edge of the bias strip and then close it over the band before sewing the fascinator base to the bias strip, using a stab stitch as close to the headband as possible to hold it securely in place. If you're using a satin- or ribbon-covered band, you don't need to use glue; instead, just catch the edge of the satin as you are sewing it inside the bias strip onto the fascinator base.

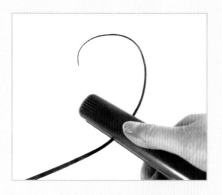

3. Next, gently curl your quills. The basic butter knife technique taught on page 36 doesn't always work with very tough quills. It is usually more effective to use heat, so you can use either a pressing iron or a hair straightener. If you are using the iron method, place the ostrich quill on an ironing board slightly padded with a cotton sheet over the board. Lay the quill rounded-side down and hold the thick end of the quill. Slowly iron the quill away from you, pressing down firmly with the iron. As you iron away, slightly pull the quill up and curl it using the edge of the iron. Repeat this process until it is as curled as you want. If using a straightener, hold the quill firmly in the straightener and slowly run it up toward the narrow end of the quill, curving the quill around as you pull it. This is a similar technique to curling a ribbon. If you are finding that the quill is breaking, try wetting it first to make it slightly more pliable. This should give each of them a nice, gentle curve at the narrow end.

4. Position the quills on the base so that the fatter ends of the quills sit just over the side of the round base. Attach them to the base by stitching them tightly in place (using double-strength thread), sewing through the quill sideways. This hides the stitches better than sewing through the top of the quill. Do the first stitch about 2½ inches (6.5 cm) from the base of the quill, and if required to stop it from wobbling, sew another stitch about 1 inch (2.5 cm) above that. Make sure you pull the thread tight each time. I recommend using a thimble or pushing the end of the needle against the surface you're working on to avoid hurting your fingers.

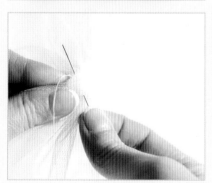

5. Take your long tulle strip(s). Using a double thickness of thread, insert your needle in one corner of the tulle. Do a running stitch, using stitches approximately ¼ inch (6 mm) apart and about ¼ inch (6 mm) long all the way along the long edge, pulling the tulle to gather it as you go. When you reach the end of the strip, pull your thread tight so that your tulle forms a large, gathered "fan," and secure with several stitches on top of each other. If you are using more than one strip, repeat this process on each strip, gathering the full length into a fan shape.

6. Join the gathered ends of the tulle strip together so that the tulle forms a complete circle. If you have used more than one strip, place them together to give the same effect. Put the gathered point(s) of the tulle in the center of the base on top of the feathers and sew this in place.

7. Take your second, smaller strip of tulle. Using the same method as in Step 5, gather the tulle along one of the long edges. Then, pull the thread very tight and secure with a few stitches.

8. Place this second tulle shape into the center of the other tulle circle, and secure it in place with a few stitches through the gathered point onto the base.

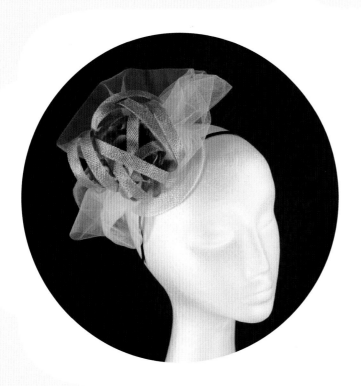

Variations

This striking piece can be varied by swapping the inner tulle for other materials, such as some sinamay bias loops, and changing the type of feathers used.

The Amelia

SINAMAY SWIRL WITH SINAMAY BIAS DETAIL

LEVEL
Intermediate

APPROXIMATE TIME TO MAKE
2 to 3 hours

MATERIALS

Approximately 15 x 25-inch (38 x 63.5 cm) rectangle of sinamay

Approximately 25 inches (63.5 cm) of ½-inch-wide (1.3 cm) sinamay bias strip in a contrasting color (page 21)

4-inch (10 cm) round or teardrop-shaped sinamay base (page 25)

3-inch (7.5 cm) sinamay bias strip at least ½ inch (1.3 cm) wider than your headband

Narrow metal- or satin-covered headband

Straight pins

Scissors

Needle and thread (colors to match sinamay and veiling)

Iron

Optional for variations: French veiling/French netting, feathers, or beads

1. Lay your rectangle of sinamay out flat. Cut it into the shape shown in the diagram on page 214. To do this, cut the two shorter ends to form an angle, changing the overall shape from a rectangle to a parallelogram. The exact angle does not matter. See the diagram on page 214 for the exact dimensions that I used.

2. You will notice that when you cut the sinamay sheet, it leaves a rough edge. To "hem" the sinamay, fold the edge over once (about ½ inch/1.3 cm) and press this all the way along each edge using your fingers, then fold that edge over on itself again by ½ inch (1.3 cm), pressing this down all the way around.

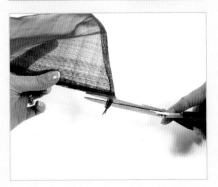

3. Trim the opposite corners that now have longer pieces of sinamay poking out to form neat corners.

4. Using a cool iron, press all the way around the double-folded edges. Now each long edge should be approximately 18 inches (45.5 cm) long and each short edge approximately 13 inches (33 cm) long.

5. Next take the midpoint of each of the short sides of the parallel-ogram in each hand and gather the sinamay. This helps to soften the stiffener in the sinamay, making it easier to manipulate and sew through.

6. The resulting shape should look like this.

7. Open up the parallelogram shape again. Secure your thread at the midpoint of one of the short sides and (using double-strength thread) do a running stitch down the center of the parallelogram, gathering the sinamay as you go.

8. Keep on gathering the sinamay, gently pulling the thread through until the two narrower ends of the parallelogram are as close together as possible, forming the same shape as you did previously in Step 6. Don't pull the thread too hard or it may snap. You can now stitch through the gathered central point several times to hold this shape in place.

9. The sinamay shape should look roughly like this.

10. Take the 25-inch (63.5 cm) sinamay bias strip. Cut the ends of the sinamay strip diagonally to give neat ends. Twist the strip around your finger and hold this in place for thirty seconds to form a twirl, and then lay this "spiral" of sinamay bias onto the sinamay shape you formed at Step 9.

11. Secure this spiral in place by doing a small stab stitch at each place that the spiral touches the sinamay shape. Use a thread that matches the color of the sinamay bias strip to hide the stitches.

12. We are now going to attach this sinamay shape that you have created to a fascinator base and an headband. Use the technique in steps 1 and 2 on page 95 to attach the headband to the fascinator base with the small sinamay bias strip.

13. Finally, place your headband with attached base on your head. Take your sinamay shape made at Step 11 and, using a mirror, place the sinamay shape on the base and turn it until you like the placement. Take it off of your head and secure your sinamay shape to the fascinator base by sewing up through the fascinator base through the gathered center point of the sinamay shape and back down again. This can be quite fiddly so you may need to stitch it several times, pulling the thread tightly each time to hold it securely in place.

Variations

This sinamay swirl idea can be made with a smaller or larger parallelogram and with different embellishments, such as French netting, feathers, and beads, which will all give very different looks.

The Thea

LARGE LACE-COVERED ROUND FASCINATOR WITH OSTRICH QUILL EMBELLISHMENT

LEVEL
Intermediate

APPROXIMATE TIME TO MAKE
4 to 6 hours

MATERIALS

12-inch round, flat sinamay base, wired and stiffened but not edged with bias or ribbon (page 27, Steps 1-4, then Step 9)

39 inches (99 cm) of ½-inch-wide (1.3 cm) sinamay bias or Petersham ribbon in a contrasting color to the sinamay

Two 12-inch (30.5 cm) circles of lace fabric

Wide satin- or ribbon-covered headband

4½-inch-long (11.5 cm) sinamay bias strip that is at least ½ inch (1.3 cm) wider than your headband

4-inch (10 cm) round fascinator base

2 ostrich quills in either matching or contrasting colors

Hair curling tongs

Pressing iron

Needle and thread

Scissors

(materials continue)

(continued)

Recommended for safety: protective/heat-resistant gloves

Optional for variations: silk butterflies, flowers, or other similar lightweight embellishments

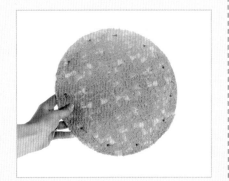

1. Once your wired and stiffened sinamay circle base is nearly dry, iron it with a cool pressing iron. Pin one circle of lace fabric onto one side of the double sinamay circle and the other onto the other side, right sides facing out. If required, trim any lace overhang outside the edge of the sinamay circle.

2. Sew the lace fabric in place by sewing it onto the sinamay circle over the edge of the wire frame using a blanket stitch (see page 19 on how to do this). Your stitches should all be just inside the wire.

3. Take your chosen edging and (following steps 5 and 6 on page 28), edge the round base using a stab stitch, making sure that you catch the fabric all the way round.

4. Heat the curling tongs, taking lots of care not to burn your hands; you can wear heat-resistant gloves to make sure you don't burn yourself. Gently wrap the thinner ends of the ostrich quills around the tongs several times. Hold for around 20 to 30 seconds, then release. This should result in some beautifully spiraled quills.

5. Position the ostrich quills where you would like them to sit. Attach them by sewing sideways through the spine of the quills with just a few stitches. You want to hide these stitches so that the feathers look like they are "floating." Sew the quill onto the base about a third of the way up the quill. If required, you can sew another stitch about 1 inch (2.5 cm) up from that. If you are finding it difficult to get your needle through the quill, use a thimble or try pushing the end of the needle against the surface you're working on.

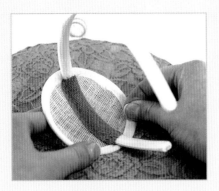

6. Attach the headband to the small fascinator base as explained in steps 1 and 2 on page 95. Position the small fascinator base with attached headband in the center of the large round disc. Use a mirror to get the right placement, then attach the small base to the large disc with a thread color that matches the lace using a stab stitch to hide the stitching. Rather than sewing all the way around the edge, sew only the lower two-thirds of the round base to the large disc so that the upper one-third of the round base can curve around the shape of your head.

Variations

This results in a really stunning fascinator that is ideal to wear to an occasion such as a cocktail party or wedding. It can be varied by leaving off the lace fabric layer and instead attaching some smaller lace appliqués or alternative embellishments like these small silk flowers.

The Eloise

SINAMAY SAUCER WITH LARGE FLOWER

LEVEL
Intermediate

APPROXIMATE TIME TO MAKE
4 hours

MATERIALS

10-inch-long (25.5 cm) oval sinamay saucer base (if you are lucky enough to have access to a saucer hat block, create a saucer base with a nice upturn; alternatively, make a flat 10-inch-long/25.5 cm oval base, following the technique on pages 27-29, Steps 1 through 6, plus Step 9

Large fabric flower (page 44), or a premade one (These can be purchased easily online: Etsy is a great source of lovely silk flowers. I used a 5½-inch/14 cm rose.)

15 inches (38 cm) French netting

4-inch (10 cm) round sinamay base (page 25)

Pronged hat elastic (these can be purchased from online millinery supply stores; alternatively, you can use a length of hat elastic—tie knots in the end and sew tightly on instead)

Needle and coordinating thread

Scissors

Optional for variations: several smaller fabric flowers, contrasting sinamay bias or Petersham ribbon for a contrasting edge

1. Make your oval fascinator base, following steps 1 through 6, plus Step 9 on pages 27-29.

2. Take the French netting and gather it in the center in a bow shape. Sew a few stitches through the gathered point to hold this in place.

3. Sew the gathered point of the netting onto the sinamay base, just off center, toward the bottom.

4. Next take the large statement fabric flower. Sew the flower onto the gathered point of the French netting. Do this by sewing through the bottom few layers of petals at the base of the flower, at a few different points around the flower. Use a matching color of thread so that your stitches are well hidden.

5. Take the small, round fascinator base and the hat elastic. Attach the elastic by poking one prong through the underside of the fascinator base, catching a few weaves on top, then back through to the underside again. The prong will then sit on the underside of the base. Repeat with the other prong on the side directly opposite the first.

6. Attach the base to the underside of the saucer base by sewing around the lower half of the round fascinator base. In the photo here I will sew the lower half of the round base that will sit against the head, from prong to prong.

Tip

Hat elastics are a great way of holding a fascinator in place. You can usually buy them in a range of colors, so look for the color closest to your own hair color when purchasing them. To wear a fascinator with a hat elastic attachment, simply slip the hat elastic under your hair at the back of your head and position the fascinator where you want it to sit. If you are wearing your hair down, simply pull some hair forward, in front of the elastic. This means that the elastic will be hidden in your hair, and you shouldn't see it at all.

Variations

Once you have mastered the technique of creating saucer, oval, and round fascinator bases, the bases can be used to create some really stunning pieces and can be embellished with flowers, feathers, lace, or sinamay shapes. Try, for example, using several smaller flowers instead of one big statement flower.

The Jasmine

SINAMAY FAN BASE WITH FRENCH NETTING DETAIL

LEVEL
Intermediate

APPROXIMATE TIME TO MAKE
4 to 6 hours

MATERIALS

Rectangular sheet of sinamay cut on the bias, 24 x 7 inches (61 x 18 cm)

34 inches (86.5 cm) millinery wire

34 inches (86.5 cm) sinamay bias strip, ¾ to 1 inch wide (2 to 2.5 cm), in a matching or contrasting color

2 colors of French netting, each approximately 16 to 20 inches (40.5 to 51 cm) long

Narrow headband, either metal or ribbon covered

Needle and thread

Scissors

Optional for variations: sinamay bias strips in a contrasting color to edge and decorate the fascinator

1. Cut out the sinamay shape as shown in the Jasmine template diagram on page 215.

2. Lay the millinery wire around the long, rounded side of the shape and attach the wire to the sinamay using a blanket stitch (see page 19 for how to do this), with your stitches about ½ inch (1.3 cm) apart. If you sew on the very edge of the sinamay it will fray, so try to sew about ¼ inch (6 mm) from the edge. Depending on how you have cut your curves, this long edge should be approximately 34 inches (86.5 cm) long.

3. Take the bias strip and check that it is long enough to go around the long, rounded side. Open up the bias strip and close it over the edge of the sinamay shape, sandwiching the sinamay and wire. Secure this all the way around using a matching color of thread and using a stab stitch.

4. Pleat the straight edge with ½- to ¾-inch (1.3 to 2 cm) pleats, creating a fan effect, guiding each fold toward the curved edge of the shape. Pinch the first 1½ to 2 inches (3.8 to 5 cm) of each pleat with your fingers to create a crease at the base of each pleat.

5. Hold the base of the pleats in place with a couple of stitches, making sure that all the cut ends are level and held together securely—don't sew the wired ends of the sinamay bias: we deal with these in the next step.

6. Next you need to secure the wired ends of the sinamay bias. To do this, pinch the wired ends of the sinamay bias so that they sit at either side of the bundle of pleats. Secure them in place with a few stitches.

7. The outer edge of your fascinator should be beginning to turn downward slightly. You can help it along by manipulating the wired edge with your fingers so that the rounded edge of your fascinator curves slightly downward.

8. Turn the fascinator upside down. Twist the bundle in a counter-clockwise direction so that the end of the bundle points toward the front of the fascinator.

9. To make sure that this stays securely in place, bind the bundle of pleats with thick thread or string and then trim the raw edges of the sinamay to give a neat end.

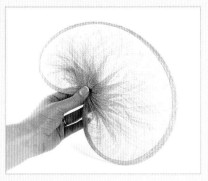

10. Turn the fascinator back over and, if necessary, rearrange the pleats so that they sit neatly by smoothing with your fingers.

11. Take each length of French netting and gather each one down the longer centerline of the netting. Sew through the gathered point to hold in place.

12. Arrange the two netting bow shapes side by side on top of the sinamay base so that they splay out over opposite sides of the sinamay base, with some of the netting overlapping over the center section of the sinamay base. The gathered point of both bows should sit on top of the gathered point of the sinamay base. Sew them in place with a few stitches.

13. To complete your fascinator, attach an headband, using the sinamay strip and the technique taught in steps 1 and 2 on page 95, to the underside of the sinamay base. Hold the netting out of the way so that this stitching does not catch the netting. Make sure you use a matching color of thread and small stab stitches so that your stitching is hidden on top of the fascinator base, although the netting will be covering it anyway.

Variations

This fascinator can be varied using contrasting color sinamay bias strips to edge the fascinator and by replacing the French netting with alternate embellishments such as sinamay bias loops attached at the gathered point.

The Sadie

SILK-COVERED PILLBOX WITH BEADING AND BIRDCAGE VEIL

LEVEL
Difficult

APPROXIMATE TIME TO MAKE
1 to 2 days (if making the base yourself)

MATERIALS

6-inch-diameter (15 cm) pillbox sinamay hat base, 1½ inches (3.8 cm) deep (page 30)

10-inch-diameter (25.5 cm) circle of silk

6 x 10½-inch (15 x 26.5 cm) rectangle of silk

Approximately 16 (¼-inch/6 mm) beads of a complementary color

27 inches (68.5 cm) French or Russian netting, 9 to 12 inches (22.8 to 32.5 cm) wide

Approximately 13 inches (33 cm) of millinery elastic

Straight pins

Iron

Optional for variations: thicker fabric such as wool, and feathers for decoration

1. Turn your pillbox hat base and lay it upside down in the center of the silk circle.

2. Turn the silk over the edge of the pillbox base and pin it in place. You will have to make very small pleats all the way around, always ensuring that you don't pull the silk too hard so that there is enough to fold over the edge of the base all the way around.

3. You may find that you have one point that has a bit of a crease on top, as I do in this photo. This happens when you're trying to cover a round shape. We can hide this crease in steps 5 and 6.

4. Sew the silk in place all the way around the inside of the hat base brim. Try to sew onto the inner side of the hat binding so that your stitching does not show on the outside of the hat. You may find that you have to trim off fabric if there is too much excess underneath. You should only have ¼ to ½ inch (6 mm to 1.3 cm) of extra silk all the way around the inside.

5. Take your rectangle of silk. Hem the long sides by folding the sides over by about ¼ inch (6 mm) and ironing down the fold with a very cool iron. Sew the folded sides down using a sewing machine or by hand with a small, neat running stitch. Lay the rectangle of silk down onto its good side (so that the hemmed side is facing up). Lay the upturned hat base on top of it. Try to position it so that any bad creases that you have on the silk already on the hat are covered by the rectangle of silk. Pin one short end of the silk rectangle along the underside of the base.

6. Turn the hat back over and twist the silk rectangle in the middle, ensuring that the twisted point is in the center of the hat. Make sure you twist it all the way around so that the good side remains pointing upward.

7. Pull it tight and pin the other short end of the rectangle in place on the underside of the base at the opposite side. Sew the two ends of the silk in place, again using the inner underside of the hat brim to sew it to. You may again find that you have to trim off fabric if there is too much underneath.

8. Sew on your beads beside the twist on top of the hat. Remember when attaching beads to double your thread to strengthen it and pull the thread tight with each stitch to avoid having any "wobbly" beads. Take an extra stitch on the underside of the hat after every few beads, so that if your thread breaks, you don't lose all your hard work.

9. Now take your French netting and make a birdcage veil using the technique taught on page 83. Attach the birdcage veil to the hat by sewing the gathered point of the birdcage veil to the middle point of the back of the hat. The birdcage veil should curve over the top of the hat.

10. If you find that the birdcage is sticking up too much instead of curving over the hat, simply put a small stitch to hold the net in place at each side of the hat, catching just one weave of the birdcage veil. I put a small stitch at the two points where my thumbs are in this photo. Use a thread that matches the color of your silk so that the stitch is hidden.

11. Pillbox hats tend to sit best when attached using millinery elastic. Millinery elastic should be attached approximately above each ear, so where exactly you attach the elastic will depend on where you want the fascinator to sit, but it will be roughly the midpoint of the pillbox base. As you have already sewn on the silk, you won't be able to use any prongs on the elastic, so simply sew it tightly on. I knotted the ends of the elastic and sewed it on securely under the knot to keep it from pulling out. Attach one side of the elastic, then place the hat on your head and use a mirror to position it as you want it to sit. It should sit toward the front of your head, slightly to one side. Once you have decided exactly where you want it to sit, pull the elastic under your hair at the back and then up again to the other side of the pillbox hat—directly opposite the point where it is already attached. Pin the elastic in place at the chosen point, and then attach it tightly in place with several stitches. Do ensure that the hat elastic is sewn firmly in place on both sides, as it will have to take quite a lot of strain when it is on your head to hold the hat in place.

Variations

This pillbox base is a great shape and very popular at the moment. It can be decorated in a number of ways: try swapping the silk for different fabrics such as thicker wool or adding a nice big bow in the same fabric.

The Emily

LARGE SAUCER FASCINATOR WITH FLOWERS AND OSTRICH QUILLS

LEVEL
Difficult

APPROXIMATE TIME TO MAKE
1 day

MATERIALS

17-inch-diameter (43 cm) sinamay saucer base or flat round base (pages 27-29, Steps 1 through 6, plus Step 9)

5 x 4-inch (12.5 x 10 cm) teardrop fascinator base

3 ostrich quills

Pressing iron or hair straightener (I used a hair straightener)

7 to 9 (1½-inch-diameter/3.8 cm) fabric flowers (this size is approximate)

Headband

5-inch (12.5 cm) strip of 1-inch-wide (2.5 cm) sinamay bias

Needle and thread

Straight pins

Scissors

Optional for variations: different feathers or sinamay to make a large sinamay bow

1. Make a large saucer base: you will need a large saucer hat block for this shape. Alternatively, you can create a slightly smaller (15-inch/38 cm) flat circular base following Steps 1 through 6, plus Step 9 on pages 27-29.

2. Next you need to gently curl your ostrich quills. I didn't want spirals, just gently curled quills like those on page 96. As explained previously, they can be quite tough, so the basic butter knife technique taught on page 37 doesn't always work. Instead, it is usually more effective to apply heat by using something such as a pressing iron or a hair straightener. To use an iron, place the ostrich quill on an ironing board slightly padded with a cotton sheet over the board. Lie the quill rounded-side down and hold the thick end of the quill. Slowly iron the quill away from you, pressing down firmly with the iron. As you press the iron gently on the quill, pull the quill up and curl it using the edge of the iron. Repeat this process until it is curled as much as you want. If using a hair straightener, hold the quill firmly in the straightener and slowly run it up the narrow end of the quill, curving the quill around as you pull it. This is a similar technique to curling a ribbon. If you are finding the quill is breaking, try wetting it first to make it slightly more pliable. This should give each of them a nice, gentle curve at the narrow end.

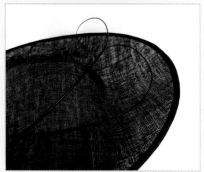

3. Next attach your quills to the outside of the saucer base by stitching them tightly in place, sewing through the quill sideways to hide your stitches. Do your stitches about a third of the way up the quill to prevent it from being wobbly. If you find they are wobbling, do another stitch about 1 inch (2.5 cm) above that. If you are finding it difficult to get your needle through the quill, try pushing the end of the needle against the surface you're working on to avoid hurting your fingers, or use a thimble to push it through.

4. Attach the second quill using the same method, positioning it at a slight angle in relation to the first quill.

5. Attach an headband to your teardrop base using the technique taught on page 95. This needs to be attached across the shorter center-line of the teardrop base.

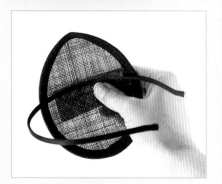

6. You now need to attach the teardrop base to the larger saucer. This is going to sit with the pointed part of the teardrop pointing to the back of the head, so use a mirror to place the small teardrop base and large saucer base on your head to ensure they are facing in the right direction, then pin the teardrop base to the saucer base. Sew the lower half of the teardrop base onto the saucer (in the photo: from my left thumb, around the bottom half over to my right thumb) using small stab stitches to ensure the stitches are hidden on the outer side of the saucer. (I've taken the photo without the headband on, for clarity, but you should already have the headband attached.)

7. Your fabric flowers are going to fill the gap between the teardrop base and the larger saucer. Pin the hat to a mannequin head to test how many flowers you are going to use and position them as you want.

8. Once you've decided how many flowers you want to use, take your fabric flowers and pin a row along the length of the visible part of the teardrop base: you'll probably fit four or five in this space. Attach these onto the teardrop base by sewing through the center of each flower and using small stab stitches. If you can't get your needle through the center of the flower, sew through some of the bottom petals instead.

9. Next fill the rest of the gap above that row with a few more flowers, sewing these onto the underside of the large saucer. Again, sew on each flower and use small stab stitches so that your stitching does not show on the upper side of the fascinator. Remember that the teardrop base will curve around your head when it is being worn, so when filling the gap with flowers remember to pull the teardrop base down as if it were sitting on your head, to check that there are no gaps that need to be filled with extra flowers.

Variations

This produces a showstopper of a hat. The large saucer base is a real statement piece that is great for society events such as going to the races or garden parties. You can vary this piece by swapping the ostrich quills for different kinds of feathers and adding some oversize sinamay embellishments such as a big sinamay bow.

The Cara

LACE-COVERED BASE WITH BURNT PHEASANT FEATHER CURLS

LEVEL
Difficult

APPROXIMATE TIME TO MAKE
1 day

MATERIALS

6-inch-diameter (15 cm) biscuit-shaped sinamay base edged in Petersham ribbon (page 32): mine is 1½ inches (3.8 cm) tall at the highest point

10-inch-diameter (25.5 cm) circle of lace fabric

6 burnt and curled pheasant feathers (page 36)

30-inch (76 cm) strip of ½-inch-wide (1.3 cm) sinamay bias

Pronged hat elastic (this can be bought from online millinery supply stores; alternatively, just use normal hat elastic and sew the knotted ends on securely to hold in place)

Needle and thread

Straight pins

Scissors

Optional for variations: taffeta or similar fabric, different feathers

1. Lay down your lace fabric circle and rest the upturned sinamay base on top of it.

2. Pull the lace fabric over the edge of the base and pin all the way around the inside edge.

3. Use a diagonal running stitch or stab stitch to hold this in place all the way around the inside edge. Sew it to the edge of the sinamay just beside the Petersham ribbon. Once sewn in place trim off any excess fabric inside the base.

4. Position your six burnt pheasant curls with three pointing upward and three pointing downward, all spread out slightly. You want the feathers to be overlapping about 2½ inches (6 cm) from their base, which is the point at which you'll sew them.

5. Attach these feathers by stitching through them sideways through the quill of the feather to hide the stitches. Avoid sewing right at the base of the feather to keep the spine from splitting, and use a fine needle.

6. Take your sinamay strip and form a double figure-8 using about 26½ inches (67.5 cm).

7. With the remaining 3½ inches (9 cm), form a small loop over the center of the figure-8. Sew this in place with a few stitches through the centerpoint.

8. Position the sinamay shape over the point at which the feathers meet. This will finish off the fascinator beautifully and also hide any stitches that are showing on the feathers. Sew it in place at the center point of the sinamay shape. If necessary, you can add another stitch or two slightly out from the center on one of the loops on each side so that the feather crossover point is covered.

9. Finally add the hat elastic. If you have pronged hat elastic, simply poke the pronged ends through the inner lip of the base or Petersham ribbon at opposite mid points of the base. If it is not pronged, tie a knot in each end of the hat elastic and tightly sew the hat elastic in place.

Variations

This style of fascinator base can be varied by covering it in a different fabric such as taffeta in place of the lace, and using different feathers instead of the pheasant curls—dyed pheasant tail feathers always give a lovely finish.

FLORAL CROWNS

The next four projects teach you to make some beautiful floral crowns. For each of these projects you can use either real or faux flowers: the same techniques can be used to attach either. There are advantages and disadvantages with both: you can simply pick real flowers from your garden, you get the benefit of the gorgeous aroma that comes with them, and, if used at a wedding, for example, you can tie them in easily with the floral displays or theme of the day. However, they obviously have a limited lifespan, they need to be refrigerated the night before use (assuming you're making them in advance), they have to be very carefully transported, and you have to be very careful when making them, as they are obviously very fragile. While faux flowers may not have the benefit of the lovely fragrance, they are more durable and slightly easier to work with, are easier to transport, have a much longer lifespan, and make a fabulous keepsake. You can also create full-on DIY projects by making the flowers yourself, meaning that you can design the exact shape, color, and size of flower that you want. If you don't want to go down the route of making all of your own flowers, there are some beautiful faux flowers available online that nowadays look very real: gone are the days of plastic-looking faux flowers. Sometimes it's actually hard to believe that well-made silk flowers aren't real! If you are purchasing faux flowers online, do be aware that the general name given to fabric flowers is "silk flowers," but they may not necessarily be made from silk. Read the description to find out what they are actually made from.

I am using faux flowers in all four of these projects, but, as I mentioned, if you would prefer to use real flowers, you can use the same techniques to create the floral crowns.

The first three of these floral crowns have a ribbon tie at the back, meaning that the size can be varied by tying the ribbon tighter or looser, so the dimensions given in each project should be suitable for most adults' heads. If you are making any of these for a child, you will need to make it smaller by using less grapevine wire. If you are making a floral crown that does not have a ribbon tie at the back but is in fact a full circle, as in project 19, you will need to measure the circumference of your head. If you are making it for someone else and can't get measurements, note that the average circumference of a female adult head is 22½ inches (57 cm).

The Summer

SUMMER DAISY FESTIVAL FLORAL CROWN

LEVEL
Easy

APPROXIMATE TIME TO MAKE
1 hour

MATERIALS

9 (2-inch/5 cm) faux daisies

Approximately 6 feet (183 cm) of florist wire

22 inches (56 cm) of grapevine wire/moss-covered craft wire (this can be purchased online in craft and florist supply stores)

2 yards (183 cm) of ribbon

Florist tape (optional)

Scissors

Optional for variations: different sizes and colors of daisies with coordinating ribbon

1. Use scissors to remove the stems of each of your daisies. Bend an 8-inch (20.5 cm) piece of florist wire in half and slide the bent point between the bottom layer of petals of the daisy so that the two ends of the wire emerge at opposite sides of the flower.

2. Twist the two ends tightly together to form a stem.

3. Place the base of one daisy approximately 4 inches (10 cm) from the end of the grapevine wire strand, and twist its wire stem around the grapevine wire to the right, keeping the wire as close to the base of the flower as possible so that the wire is hidden behind a daisy.

4. Repeat this process for all nine flowers, leaving a gap of about 1½ inches (3.8 cm) between flowers. Make sure you leave 4 inches (10 cm) between the last flower and the end of the grapevine wire. When attaching the final flower, wrap the wire to the left rather than the right so that it's hidden behind a flower.

5. Create a loop with the end of the grapevine wire and wrap the end of the grapevine wire back on itself, behind the final daisy. Repeat this on the other side. You can keep the grapevine and wire from catching your hair or scratching your head by wrapping the grapevine in florist's tape in between the flowers. This will mask any sharp ends. (See step 9 on page 154 for more detail.)

6. Cut the ribbon in half. Fold a 1-yard (91.5 cm) length in half and poke the folded section through the grapevine wire loop on one side of the crown, feeding the ribbon back through the ribbon loop. Repeat on the other side with the second piece of ribbon. This can now be tied to secure the crown on your head.

Variations

This gorgeous summery floral crown is perfect
for wearing to festivals or summer parties, or for
bridesmaids. You can make a smaller version for children.
It can be varied using different sizes and colors of flowers to
produce some very different looks. In the variation, I simply
swapped the yellow daisies for some larger jade daisies.

The Mia

SWEETHEART MINIATURE ROSE FLORAL CROWN

LEVEL
Easy

APPROXIMATE TIME TO MAKE
2 hours

MATERIALS

40 faux miniature (1-inch/2.5 cm) sweetheart roses in three different shades of the same color (if your roses are larger or smaller, plan on fewer or more flowers)

Approximately 8 feet (244 cm) of florist wire

22 inches (56 cm) of grapevine wire/moss-covered craft wire (this can be purchased online in craft and florist supply stores)

2 yards (183 cm) of ribbon

Florist tape

Scissors

Optional for variations: larger faux anemones with coordinating ribbon

1. Use scissors to remove the stems of each of your miniature roses. Thread a 4-inch (10 cm) piece of florist wire through the center of a flower and create a hook at the end. Pull this back through the flower so that the hook catches the center of each flower.

2. Repeat this process for all of your miniature roses. You'll need between 30 and 40 roses, depending on how big your flowers are and how full and long you want this floral crown to look.

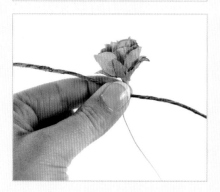

3. To form the crown, place the base of one rose approximately 4 inches (10 cm) from the end of the grapevine wire strand.

4. Secure the rose to the grapevine wire by wrapping the rose's stem around the grapevine wire, wrapping to the right.

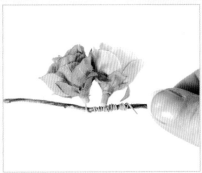

5. Add the second rose using the same technique. Make sure it is very close to the first one.

6. Continue using this process, overlapping some of the flowers by having some sticking out from the grapevine wire more than others to form clusters of roses. Don't worry about the twisted wire on the grapevine wire; this should all be hidden from sight by the roses.

7. Repeat this process until the flowers reach about 4 inches (10 cm) from the other end. When attaching the final two flowers, wrap the wire to the left rather than the right so that it's hidden among the flowers.

8. Create a loop with the end of the grapevine wire and wrap the end of the grapevine wire back on itself, behind the roses. Repeat this on the other side.

9. One option to avoid the wire catching in your hair or scratching you, and to make the crown more comfortable, is to wrap the grapevine-wire base between the flowers with floral tape. This will mask any sharp wire ends.

10. Cut the ribbon in half. Fold a 1-yard (91.5 cm) length in half and poke the folded section through the wire loop on one side of the crown, feeding the ribbon back through the ribbon loop. Repeat on the other side. This can now be tied to secure the crown on your head.

Variations

This simple floral crown can be varied using blooms of different sizes and shapes to produce some very different looks. In our variation here, we have swapped the miniature roses for some larger faux anemones.

The Olivia

ROMANTIC PASTEL FLORAL CROWN

LEVEL
Easy

APPROXIMATE TIME TO MAKE
2 hours

MATERIALS

1 large bunch of real or faux baby's breath

4 faux anemones

Approximately 10 small bunches of miniature roses

Approximately 8 feet (244 cm) of florist wire

22 inches (56 cm) of grapevine wire or rustic craft wire, or moss-covered wire (available in most craft stores)

2 yards (183 cm) of ribbon (approximately ½ inch/1 cm wide)

2 yards (183 cm) of lace (approximately ½ inch/1 cm wide)

Florist tape (optional)

Scissors

Optional for variations: different-color flowers, plus coordinating ribbons

1. Cut short, 2- to 4-inch (5 to 10 cm) sprigs of baby's breath from the larger stems. I used fifteen of these in total.

2. Place the first sprig of baby's breath 4 inches (10 cm) from the end of the grapevine wire and secure it in place by wrapping a 6-inch (15 cm) length of florist wire around the base of the baby's breath stem a few times, then wrapping the two ends of the florist wire together, and securing them by wrapping around the grapevine wire until the florist wire is used up.

3. Take another sprig of baby's breath and overlap the first one, covering up the green stems. Repeat Step 2 to secure to the grapevine wire.

4. Repeat this for all of the baby's breath, finishing about 4 inches (10 cm) from the other end of the grapevine wire.

5. Take one small bunch of your miniature roses. Take a 6-inch (15 cm) length of florist wire and wrap this around tightly below the miniature rose heads, twisting the two ends of the wire together.

6. Position the roses among the baby's breath and wrap the twisted wire around the baby's breath and grapevine wire, hiding the twisted wire among the baby's breath as much as possible. Repeat for all the bunches of roses, spreading them out around the crown.

7. Take one of your anemones and a 10-inch (25.5 cm) length of florist wire. Pull back some of the bottom layer of petals and slip the midpoint of the wire on top of those petals.

8. Pull the wire back and twist the two ends of the wire together under the flower.

9. Use this twisted wire to attach the anemone to the crown by twisting it around the grapevine wire and flowers, hiding the wire as much as possible among the other flowers.

10. Repeat for all the anemones. Spread the anemones around the crown; if you have any areas where a lot of wire is showing, cover the wire with the anemones.

11. Create a loop with the end of the grapevine wire and wrap the end around the grapevine wire toward the flowers. Repeat on the other side. You can keep the grapevine and wire from catching your hair or scratching your head by wrapping the grapevine in florist's tape in between the flowers. This will mask any sharp ends. (See step 9 on page 154 for more detail.)

12. Cut the ribbon and lace in half. Take 1 yard (91.5 cm) each of ribbon and lace. Hold them together and pull the ends through the loop and secure with a knot. Repeat on the other side with the remaining ribbon and lace.

Variations

This is one of my favorite floral crowns, as it
gives such a beautiful, romantic look. Adding
lace to the ribbon gives it a real Bohemian feel. Simply
change the types and color of larger flowers among the baby's
breath to give a different feel to it. As with all of the floral
crowns in this book, you can use either real or faux flowers:
the same techniques work for both.

The Isla

ELEGANT FLORAL CROWN WITH PEARL DRAPES

LEVEL
Intermediate

APPROXIMATE TIME TO MAKE
3 hours

MATERIALS

11 faux delphinium blossoms, approximately 1½ inches (3.8 cm) wide

Approximately 77.5 inches (197 cm) of grapevine or rustic craft wire, or moss-covered wire (available in most craft stores)

Approximately 6 feet (183 cm) of florist wire

Approximately 36 inches (91.5 cm) of bead-stringing wire (I used 0.015 inch/0.38 mm diameter Beadalon wire)

Approximately 200 (6 mm) pearl beads

Measuring tape

Scissors

4 (2 mm) crimping beads

Flat nose pliers

Optional for variations: different flowers, different beads instead of pearls

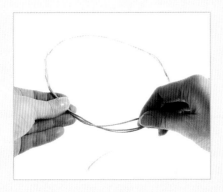

1. Take your measuring tape and measure the circumference of your head where you want the floral crown to sit. Don't pull it too tightly around your head when measuring. When you have established what this figure is (mine is 22½ inches/56 cm, so it's likely to be close to that measurement for most adult heads with hair), multiply it by 3 and add on 10 inches (25.5 cm) (for my 22½-inch/56 cm head example, the total length will be 77½ inches/197 cm). Cut that length of grapevine wire. Form a loop with the grapevine wire that is equal to the measurement you took of the circumference of your head. Now wrap the grapevine wire over itself to secure the loop. The first few wraps should be quite tight to ensure it is fixed in place, and then start gently wrapping the wire all the way around the main loop. When you have reached your starting point, keep wrapping and go around a second time, continually wrapping the grapevine wire as you go. This will form the base of your floral crown.

2. If you are using faux flowers, as I am, use scissors to remove the stems of each of your delphiniums. Thread a 5-inch (12.5 cm) piece of florist wire through the center of each delphinium and create a hook at the end.

3. Secure the wired delphinium to the grapevine wire by wrapping the wire around the grapevine wire. When wrapping, keep the wraps close to the base of the flower so that they are hidden from view as much as possible.

4. Add a second and third delphinium, using the same technique. Make sure they are very close together, in a cluster.

5. Leave a gap of 3 inches (7.5 cm), then repeat steps 3 and 4 to create another cluster of flowers, this time using two flowers. Repeat steps 3 and 4 another three times, each time varying the number of flowers at each point (use between one and three flowers each time), and each time leaving approximately 2 to 3 inches (5 to 7.5 cm) between the clusters.

6. Thread two crimping beads onto your beading wire. Wrap the end of the beading wire around the grapevine loop near a cluster of flowers. Thread the end of the wire back through the two crimping beads (so that there is now a double thickness of wire in the crimping beads) and secure them by squeezing the crimping beads closed using the flat nose pliers.

7. Thread on enough pearl beads to fill about 32 inches (81 cm) of the beading wire. Hold tightly onto the unsecured end of the beading wire at all times to make sure you don't drop it.

8. Keep holding on to the end of the string of pearls, and wrap the beading wire loosely around the crown, draping it six times, with the drapes spaced out around the whole circumference of the crown. Don't worry just now if the drapes aren't even lengths: you'll perfect this in the next step.

9. Once you have wrapped the string of pearls around the crown, secure the end of the beading wire as you did at the other end by threading on two crimping beads, looping the beading wire around the grapevine wire, passing the end back through the two crimping beads, and securing them by squeezing them closed using the flat nose pliers.

10. Now that the string of pearls is secured, you can play around with the drapes until you have them sitting as you wish. Do this by just moving the string of pearls until it is draping fairly evenly all the way around the crown. When you have it positioned as you want, use some small lengths of florist wire to attach the string of pearls to the grapevine wire at the points it touches. Just wrap the wire once between two pearls at each point and twist the ends a couple of times to hold it in place, then cut off any excess wire.

Variations

As with all the floral crown projects, you can really change the look of each design by swapping the types or just the color of flowers that you use. With this design you can also swap the pearls for other colors of beads and crystals.

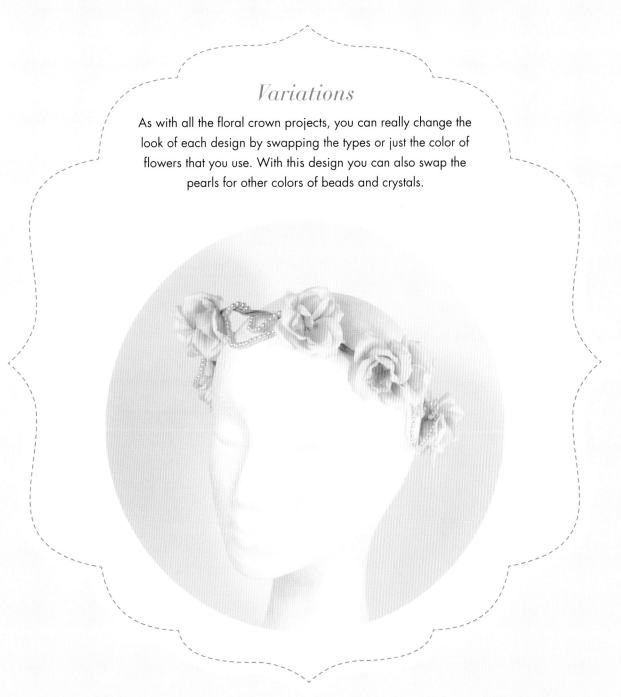

The next two projects teach you how to make lovely wire- and bead-based tiaras. Silver-plated wire, or silver-coated wire, is really fun to work with. Once you buy some very basic tools—wire cutters, flat nose pliers, wire, crimping beads, and beads—you can have fun making a huge variety of designs, experimenting with different thicknesses of wire to allow you to make more structured shapes. Here I have designed one "traditional" tiara shape, great for a bridal, prom, or pageant tiara, and one less-structured wire fascinator that is really versatile and could either be worn for a special occasion or simply on a day-to-day basis. You'll see that I've made a variation on each piece, too, to give you some ideas for other tiaras and fascinators that you can make following these projects. One safety note: When cutting wire, be very careful not to cut your fingers with the wire cutters, and also beware that bits of wire can fly up into your eyes when you cut them. If you haven't worked with craft wire before, you may want to wear some simple safety goggles.

The Isabella

SILVER WIRE, SWAROVSKI CRYSTAL BEAD, AND PEARL TIARA

LEVEL
Intermediate

APPROXIMATE TIME TO MAKE
3 to 4 hours

MATERIALS

22-gauge (0.6 mm) silver-plated wire

Tiara band or narrow metal headband

39 (¼-inch/6 mm) pearl beads

36 (⅛-inch/4 mm) pearl beads

36 silver-lined clear seed beads

5 (8 mm) Swarovski bicone clear crystal beads

15 (¼-inch/6 mm) Swarovski bicone clear crystal beads

Round and flat nose pliers

Small craft wire cutters

Optional for variations: Variety of beads

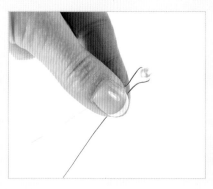

1. Cut two 8-inch (20.5 cm) lengths of the silver wire. Feed one of the larger pearl beads onto one of the wires until it is halfway along the wire and fold the wire over the bead.

2. Twist the wire tightly four times to hold it in place, then feed on a smaller crystal to one strand of the wire and again twist the wire four times beneath it to hold it in place.

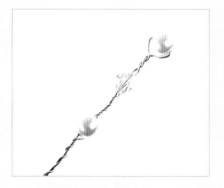

3. Finally, feed on another larger pearl bead to one strand of wire, then twist the wire tightly under the pearl to hold this in place. Continue twisting until the wire is used up.

4. Repeat steps 1 to 3 so you have two matching stems. Make sure the pearl beads and crystals sit at the same level on each stem.

5. Repeat steps 1 to 4, but this time using two 10-inch (25.5 cm) lengths of silver wire, and do seven twists between each bead so that the resulting strands are slightly longer than the first pair. Then repeat steps 1 to 4 again, but this time use two 12-inch (30.5 cm) lengths of silver wire and do ten twists between each bead so that the resulting strands are slightly longer than the first four. You should now have three pairs of stems with each pair being a slightly different length.

6. Now repeat the above steps 1 to 5, but this time swap the pearl-crystal-pearl configuration for a crystal-pearl-crystal configuration so that you have a larger crystal at the top, then a larger pearl bead, then a smaller crystal. Make one stem of the longest length, one pair of the medium length, and one pair of the shorter length.

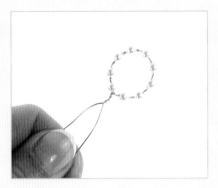

7. Next you need to make the final style of stem. For this style, cut a 10-inch (25.5 cm) length of silver wire. Take nine small pearl beads and nine seed beads. Thread on alternating pearl beads and seed beads, and then twist them into a loop. Now twist the wire three times to hold the loop in place.

8. Feed on a smaller crystal, twist the wire three times, then a larger pearl bead, then twist the wire to the end of the wire. Repeat steps 7 and 8 three times so that you have four loops.

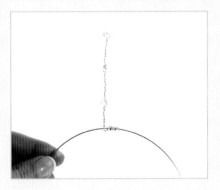

9. You should now have a grand total of eleven stems and four loops. Find the central point of your tiara band or headband. Take your single, long crystal-pearl-crystal stem and use the excess wire to twist this onto the band at the central point.

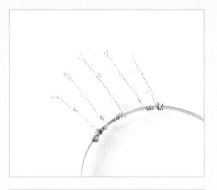

10. Take your pair of longest pearl-crystal-pearl stems and twist them onto the band at each side of the longer stem, approximately ⅓ inch (8 mm) away from it. Make sure that the top pearl sits slightly lower than the central top crystal. Next twist on the longest pair of crystal-pearl-crystal stems, again about ⅓ inch (8 mm) from the previous stems and, again ensuring that the top crystals sit slightly lower than the top pearls on the stems next to them.

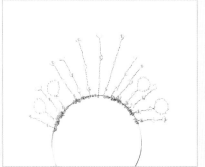

11. Twist on the rest of your stems in order of descending length. The order the rest are attached should be (1) pearl-crystal-pearl, (2) pearl/crystal loop, (3) crystal-pearl-crystal, (4) pearl/crystal loop, and (5) pearl crystal-pearl. The tiara will look prettier if you reposition the stems so that they splay outward a little from the center.

12. Finally, to hide some of the wire wrapped around the tiara or headband, cut off 24 inches (61 cm) of silver wire. Wrap the silver wire around the band between the last two stems on the left of the tiara, then feed on two pearls to the left of all the stems. Continue to wrap the wire between the stems, feeding on one pearl bead to sit between each stem, finishing with two at the right-hand side of all the stems to match the left-hand side. This will use up the remaining eighteen pearl beads.

Variations

This tiara project can be varied by adding some
colored beads into the design, using larger beads, or mixing
up the configurations of crystals and beads that you're using.
Try doing more loops or making some shapes with thicker wire
instead of having straight lines. There really are
endless possibilities with this tiara style!

The Anna

ELEGANT SILVER WIRE AND PEARL SIDE TIARA

LEVEL
Intermediate

APPROXIMATE TIME TO MAKE
3 to 4 hours

MATERIALS

¼-inch (6 mm) silver metal headband

Approximately 85 inches (216 cm) of 20-gauge (0.8 mm) silver-plated wire

Approximately 44 inches (112 cm) of 22-gauge (0.6 mm) silver-plated wire

Approximately 150 (¼- to ⅓-inch-long/6 to 8 mm) oval pearl beads (make sure the holes in the beads are big enough to take the silver-plated wire)

Small strip of masking or craft tape

Small craft wire cutters

Optional for variations: colored beads

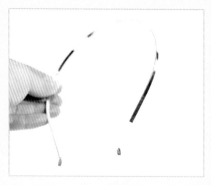

1. Put the headband on your head. Decide which side of your head you want the main design to sit, then use the masking tape to mark the headband at the point where the top of your ear is on that side of your head. You don't want the pearl design to go down further than your ear. You can also mark where you want the design to stop on the other side of your head.

2. Cut an 8-inch (20 cm) length of 20-guage (0.8 mm) silver wire. Feed it through one pearl bead and wrap it back on itself to secure that bead at the end of the wire.

3. Feed on sixteen more pearl beads. You should have about 2 inches (5 cm) of wire left unbeaded.

4. Now curl this beaded wire into a spiral shape. Once you have formed the spiral, wrap the 2 inches (5 cm) of unbeaded wire once around the wire between the end two beads to hold the spiral shape in place. Put this aside and repeat steps 2 to 4 twice more so that you have three equal-sized pearl spirals, again with a 2-inch (5 cm) unbeaded length of wire at the end.

5. Cut an 11-inch (28 cm) length of wire. Repeat steps 2 to 4, but this time feed on twenty-five pearl beads so that the resulting spiral is a bit larger than the first three (and only make one spiral).

6. Cut a 13-inch (33 cm) length of wire. Repeat steps 2 to 4, but this time feed on thirty-one pearl beads so that you have one even larger pearl spiral, again with a 2-inch (5 cm) unbeaded length of wire at the end. You should now have three small, one medium, and one large pearl spirals.

7. You now need to fix these spirals to the headband using the 2-inch (5 cm) unbeaded length of wire at the end of each spiral. Do this by simply placing one of the smaller spirals on the headband about 2½ inches (6.5 cm) above the masking tape that was at the top of your ear. Tightly wrap the unbeaded wire around the headband. Make sure that the end of the wire is tucked over the top of the headband, and is hidden under the pearl spiral. This is to make sure that the end doesn't catch in your hair or scratch your head.

8. Next, position another of the smaller three spirals just above and very close to the first spiral but on the opposite side of the headband. Wrap the unbeaded wire stem tightly around the headband to hold it in place. Remember to tuck the end of the wire onto the topside of the headband under a spiral.

9. Repeat this process, alternating sides with each spiral. Start with the largest spiral, then the medium spiral, and ending with the final, smaller one.

10. You can now finish the design by covering the rest of the headband down to each ear with a simple row of pearls. Start with the side where there is less headband showing. Take 12 inches (30.5 cm) of 22-gauge (0.6 mm) silver wire and wrap it several times tightly around the headband under one of the pearl spirals at the edge of the design, catching the end of the wire tightly under four or five wraps to hold it in place.

11. Wrap the wire down to where the masking tape is, each time feeding on a pearl so that it sits diagonally across the headband. You will need around ten to twelve pearl beads, depending on where exactly your design starts and how far up the headband your masking tape is.

12. When you reach the masking tape, wrap the wire three times around the headband below the final pearl bead, before tucking the end of the wire in between the last two pearl beads. Repeat this on the other side. You will need about 32 inches (81.5 cm) of wire and about twenty-five to thirty beads for this side, as there will be more headband to cover.

13. Finally, remove the masking tape and your beautiful pearl side tiara is finished.

Variations

Play around with the shapes: try making some flower shapes instead of spirals, or use colored beads to tie in with your outfit. Here I bent the wire into a nice flower shape and swapped the pearl beads for purple beads to create a lovely, everyday use side tiara that can be worn by children or adults.

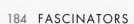

The next two projects teach you how to make a couple of beautiful, simple bridal fascinators. These fascinators look lovely with a range of bridal dress styles and can be easily adapted to tie in with the detail on your dress. Feel free to swap the pearls for sparkling crystal beads if you are opting for sparkle instead of pearl on your big day, add a splash of color by using some colored lace or beads if your dress or other bridal accessories are a particular color, or make them larger or smaller depending on the look you're going for. I have also included some variations to show how easy it is to adapt these fascinators for a very different look.

The Vivienne

BRIDAL LACE AND PEARL FASCINATOR

LEVEL
Easy

APPROXIMATE TIME TO MAKE
2 hours

MATERIALS

Approximately 30 inches (76 cm) of 3-inch-wide (7.5 cm) scalloped-edge lace

Needle and coordinating thread

Approximately 30 pearl beads (I used ¼-inch/6 mm beads)

3-inch-diameter (7.5 cm) circle of white or ivory felt

27 inches (68.5 cm) of 9-inch-wide (23 cm) ivory French netting

Straight pins

Barrette/crocodile clip or 2-inch (5 cm) comb (the comb can be plastic or metal)

A bobby pin (also called a Kirby grip)

Hot glue gun (only required if using a clip rather than a comb)

Optional for variations: soft tulle fabric or an headband

1. Take your scalloped lace and start gathering it in a spiral formation, holding on to the center point with one hand. Keep on spiraling this around until you have used all of your lace.

2. Pin this in place. If you have used 3-inch-wide (7.5 cm) lace, this spiral should be about 5 inches (12.5 cm) wide at the widest point. Sew this in place by sewing back and forth through all the layers in the center.

3. Next sew the pearl beads onto the front center of the spiral: not only does this look pretty, but also it will cover any mess made when sewing the lace in place. Take your pearl beads and sew them on individually, bringing the needle from the back to the front, adding a bead, then putting the needle back down through the center again.

4. Repeat this process, building the pile of beads up until the entire untidy lace center is covered and you have a nice cluster of beads in the center.

5. Now turn the lace spiral over so that it is upside down. Take your circle of felt and lay it on the back of the lace spiral, in the center. Hold it here and turn the fascinator back over to check that the felt cannot be seen from the front; it should be hidden by the lace, so if necessary trim it down a bit.

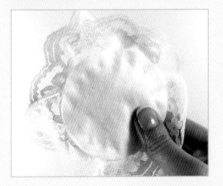

6. Once the felt circle is the correct size, pin the felt circle in place. You can now sew it in place by doing a small running stitch around the circle, approximately ¼ inch (6 mm) in from the edge, to secure it to the back layer of the lace spiral.

7. Next attach your crocodile clip or comb across the felt circle. If using a crocodile clip, you can just hot glue this on. If using a comb, sew it on as we have in previous projects (see page 58, for example).

8. You now need to make a birdcage veil. Take your length of French netting. Lay it down lengthwise and cut off the top two corners—approximately 4 inches (10 cm) along the edge to create the shape shown in the Birdcage Veil template on page 213.

9. Using a needle and thread, secure your thread in the bottom corner of the netting (point X in the diagram). Weave the thread in and out of the diamonds of the netting all the way around the edge of the netting, apart from the long, uncut edge—weaving along sides A, B, C, D, and E in the diagram.

10. Once you have woven the thread through all the diamonds, pull it tight. This will gather the netting to form a birdcage veil. Secure this shape with a few stitches through the gathered part of the birdcage veil (points X and Y in the diagram are now pulled together).

Tip

To wear this piece, simply put your bobby pin through the gathered point of the birdcage veil and secure it in your hair, using a mirror to position the birdcage veil wherever you want it to sit. Then, take your lace fascinator and secure this in your hair, fixing it on right behind the gathered point of the birdcage veil so that the gathered point is covered up.

Variations

To vary this, try swapping the lace for some soft tulle to give it more body, gathering it into a larger, puffier spiral shape.

The Carly

BRIDAL FLORAL ORGANZA FASCINATOR

LEVEL
Easy

APPROXIMATE TIME TO MAKE
2 hours

MATERIALS

4-inch (10 cm) round sinamay base in the chosen color (I used ivory, but you can choose whatever color matches the dress)

3-inch-wide (7.5 cm) plastic or metal comb

6-inch (15 cm) circle of lace

Straight pins

Paper and pencil

10 x 10-inch (25.5 x 25.5 cm) piece of organza fabric (in the same color as the base)

5 x 5-inch (13 x 13 cm) piece of tulle netting (in the same color as the organza and base)

Approximately 17 (⅛-inch/3 mm) small pearl beads

1. Attach the comb to the underside of your round base using the method taught in previous projects (see page 58, for example).

2. Take your round sinamay base and lay it upside down on top of your circle of lace. Fold the edge of the lace over the edge of the sinamay base and pin in place on the underside of the base.

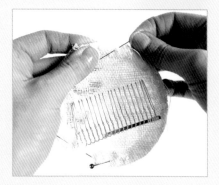

3. Sew this in place by sewing all the way around, onto the edge of the underside of the base.

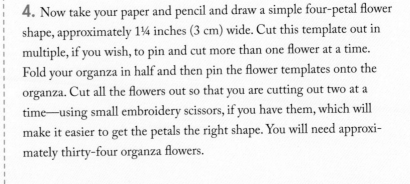

4. Now take your paper and pencil and draw a simple four-petal flower shape, approximately 1¼ inches (3 cm) wide. Cut this template out in multiple, if you wish, to pin and cut more than one flower at a time. Fold your organza in half and then pin the flower templates onto the organza. Cut all the flowers out so that you are cutting out two at a time—using small embroidery scissors, if you have them, which will make it easier to get the petals the right shape. You will need approximately thirty-four organza flowers.

5. Using the same paper templates, pin them onto the tulle fabric. Cut out the tulle flowers: you'll need seventeen of them. Arrange the organza and tulle flowers in piles, sandwiching a tulle flower between two organza flowers so you have lots of piles of three flowers.

6. Take one pile and sew it onto the lace-covered fascinator base. Start by bringing your needle up from underneath, sewing through the center of the three-layer organza-tulle-organza flower and putting a bead on top in the center of the flower, before putting the needle back down through the center of the flower.

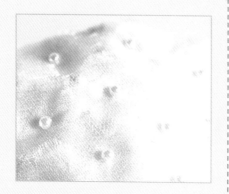

7. Now place another flower pile next to the one you have just sewn on and repeat Step 6. Do this until the base is completely covered. Don't worry if you find that there are some little gaps between flowers, as the lace underneath will show through and look pretty in any gaps.

Variations

You can vary this by using small faux flowers instead of the organza and tulle flowers, and by adding some embellishment such as a piece of netting to form a mini-birdcage veil.

Finally, I show you how to make a couple of cute, fun children's fascinators. My own daughter loves these, and they look great if you make them to tie in with the color of a dress or special outfit. These projects are a great way to use up any old scraps of fabric, felt, and ribbon that you have lying around the house.

The Milly

CUTE CHILDREN'S CRIN AND NETTING BOW

LEVEL
Easy

APPROXIMATE TIME TO MAKE
1 to 2 hours

MATERIALS

24 inches (61 cm) of 2-inch-wide (5 cm) horsehair (crin)

15 inches (38 cm) of 2-inch-wide (5 cm) horsehair (crin) (in a different, complementary color)

10 inches (25.5 cm) of 9-inch-wide (23 cm) French netting in a complementary color

A few colorful buttons to embellish the center of the bow

Satin/fabric-covered headband (at least ½ inch/1 cm wide; in a complementary color)

2-inch (5 cm) circle of felt (ideally in a complementary color, but you don't see much of this anyway)

Straight pins

Needle and thread

Scissors

Fabri-Tac glue or a hot glue gun

Optional for variations: printed cotton fabric, felt fabric

1. Cut off 18 inches (45.5 cm) from the 24-inch (61 cm) length of crin. Use this to form a bow shape by folding over the two ends to meet in the center, overlapping slightly. Pin this in place.

2. Form a second bow with the shorter, 15-inch (38 cm) strip of crin in a different color. Place the two bows of crin on top of each other. Remove the pins, then pinch the center point slightly with your fingers. Stitch the two bows together in the center point to hold this in place.

3. Take the 6-inch (15 cm) strip of crin that was left over at Step 1 and pin one end of it to the underside of the double bow.

4. Wrap the crin tightly around the center of the bow twice, fold the end underneath itself to hide any frayed ends, and sew this end to the underside of the bow.

5. Add any embellishments that you would like in the center of the bow. I am sewing on three small buttons.

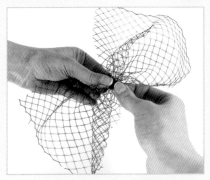

6. Take the French netting and gather it down the centerline, using your hands, then stitch the gathered point of the netting to secure.

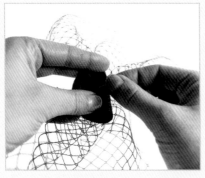

7. Take the circle of felt and sew the gathered point of the French netting onto it.

8. Sew the crin bow to the felt circle, on top of the French netting.

9. Using either your Fabri-Tac glue or hot glue gun (taking care not to burn your fingers if using the hot glue gun), attach the felt circle to the headband by applying some glue to the outside of the band at the point where you want the bow to sit (usually about one-third of the way around the band) and sticking the felt circle and bow on. Then apply some glue to the underside of the band at the point where the bow sits, and fold one side of the felt around the headband and stick it down with the glue.

10. Apply some more glue to the underside of the felt before folding over and sticking down the other side of the felt circle.

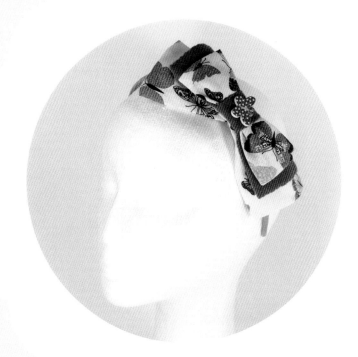

Variations

You can vary this piece by using some nice printed cotton fabric or felt instead of crin— it's a great way to use up any small pieces of fabric you have lying around and jazz up any boring, plain headbands your little one has!

The Lola

CHILDREN'S COLORFUL 3D FELT FLOWER HEADBAND

LEVEL
Intermediate

APPROXIMATE TIME TO MAKE
3 to 4 hours

MATERIALS

Photocopies or sketches on paper of the templates on page 216

Pieces of felt in a range of colors, including yellows, greens, pinks, and blues

Straight pins

Needle and thread

Scissors

Felt balls (about ½ inch/1 cm diameter)

Buttons

35 inches (89 cm) of 1-inch-wide (2.5 cm) ribbon

Optional for variations: different colors of felt, different fabrics

1. Use the templates on page 216 as a guide to the flower and leaf shapes. You can photocopy these or just copy them by hand: don't worry if they're not exactly the same. These are just a guide for the general shape of the flowers and leaves.

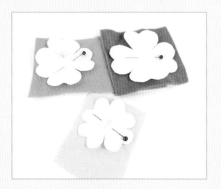

2. Cut out three paper templates of flower A in three sizes: one 3-inch diameter (7.5 cm), one 2½-inch diameter (6.5 cm), and one 2-inch diameter (5 cm). These will make the three layers for the first flower. Choose your felt colors: the three layers could be the same color or three different shades of a color, as I have used. Pin on the templates to the felt and cut out the flower shapes.

3. Starting with the largest layer, fasten on your thread at the base of one petal and make a small circle of running stitches in the center of the flower. The circle should be about ¼ inch (6 mm) in diameter.

4. When you reach the point where you started the stitches, pull the thread so that the center of the flower shape gathers a little. Push the center of the flower down as you gather. Fasten off your thread with a couple of small stitches. Repeat this for each layer of the flower.

5. Place the layers together, the largest at the bottom and the smallest on the top. Rotate each layer to ensure that the petals of each layer are showing, and stitch through the center of all three layers a couple of times to hold them together. You can twist some of the petals so they stand up a little, to give more shape to the flower.

6. Sew a button to the center of the flower.

7. Follow steps 2 to 6 above for flower B, using a different range of colors. For flower C, choose the same templates as for flower A, but make the flowers 2½ inches (6.5 cm), 2 inches (5 cm), and 1½ inches (3.8 cm), and repeat steps 2 through 6. Repeat this to make two of flower C. Instead of button centers, you can make felt ball centers, using the method in step 10.

8. Use template D to cut out the shape in felt. Fold up about ½ inch (1.3 cm) of the felt (where the dotted line is drawn on the template) along the bottom and then roll the strip around your finger, with the folded layer inside, until the side edges meet. Sew these edges neatly together, making a tube shape.

9. Now make a series of running stitches around the folded edge at the bottom and pull these to gather the bottom of the tube tightly, making a cup-shaped flower. Fasten the thread firmly.

10. Choose a small felt ball. Fasten your thread on the underside of the flower, push the needle through to the inside of the cup shape and take it out of the top. Pass the needle through the felt ball (sideways so that the stitch does not show on top) and then back down again through the base of the flower, pulling the ball down into the cup to form a center for the flower.

11. Use the template for flower E to cut out two of the petal shapes in the same color of felt, both 2½ inches (6.5 cm) in diameter, and a small circle to go in the center of the flower. Make a circle of running stitches in the middle of each layer of petals, pulling the thread to gather the center in. Stitch the two layers together in the center. Now rest the circle in the center of the top layer and stitch in place. Fasten off here, and then sew a button, bead, or sequin to the center on the top of the center circle. Repeat this process so that you have two of flower E.

12. For the leaves, use the leaf templates to cut out three of leaf type 1 and two of leaf type 2. For the base, cut out an oblong shape of felt approximately 10 inches (25.5 cm) long and 3 inches (7.5 cm) wide.

13. Assemble the flowers as shown, stitching each flower and leaf in place on the base, working from the center out toward each side.

14. Attach this whole piece to the 1-inch-wide (2.5 cm) ribbon using a simple running stitch around the base, attaching it to the ribbon. Your stitches should be hidden under the felt flowers. To secure onto the head, this can be tied at the back, under the hair.

Variations

There are lots of ways to make pretty variations of this piece. Try playing around with the shape and color of the flowers and use different fabrics instead of felt or mixed in with the felt.

Template: Rose Petals

NOT TO SCALE: PRINT AT 125%

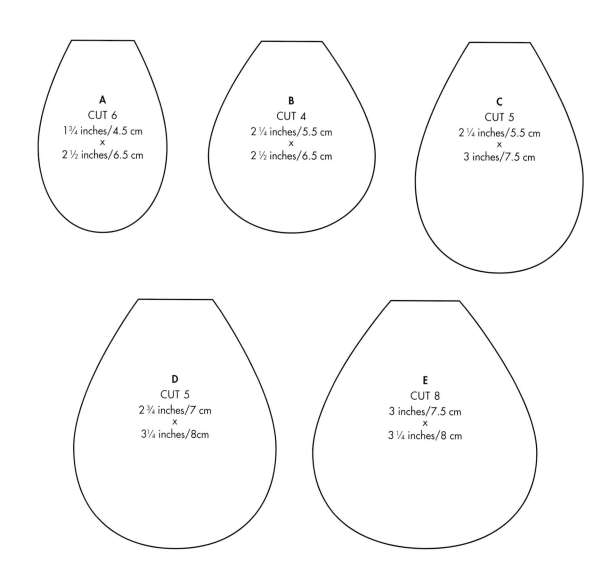

A
CUT 6
1 ¾ inches/4.5 cm
x
2 ½ inches/6.5 cm

B
CUT 4
2 ¼ inches/5.5 cm
x
2 ½ inches/6.5 cm

C
CUT 5
2 ¼ inches/5.5 cm
x
3 inches/7.5 cm

D
CUT 5
2 ¾ inches/7 cm
x
3 ¼ inches/8cm

E
CUT 8
3 inches/7.5 cm
x
3 ¼ inches/8 cm

Template: Birdcage Veil

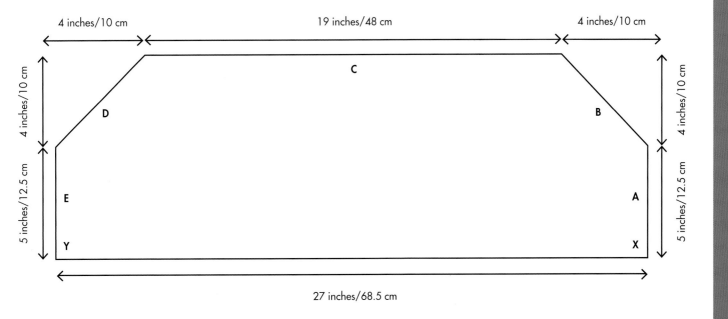

4 inches/10 cm

19 inches/48 cm

4 inches/10 cm

4 inches/10 cm

4 inches/10 cm

5 inches/12.5 cm

5 inches/12.5 cm

C

D

B

E

A

Y

X

27 inches/68.5 cm

Template: Project 9

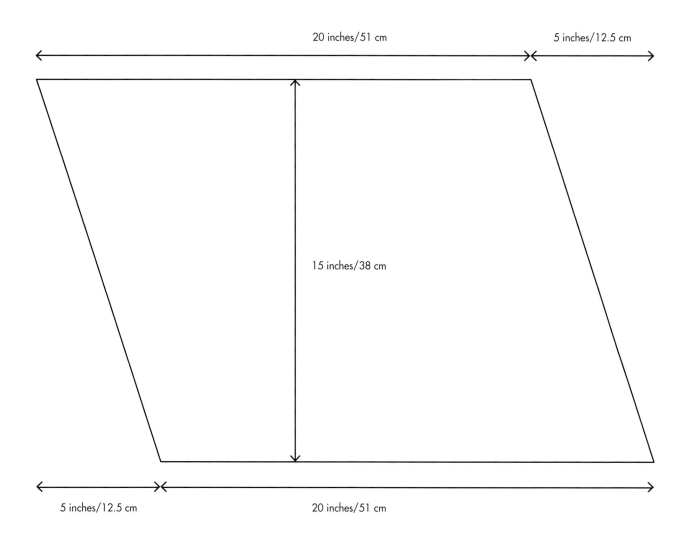

20 inches/51 cm   5 inches/12.5 cm

15 inches/38 cm

5 inches/12.5 cm   20 inches/51 cm

Template: Project 12

24 inches/61 cm

7 inches/18 cm

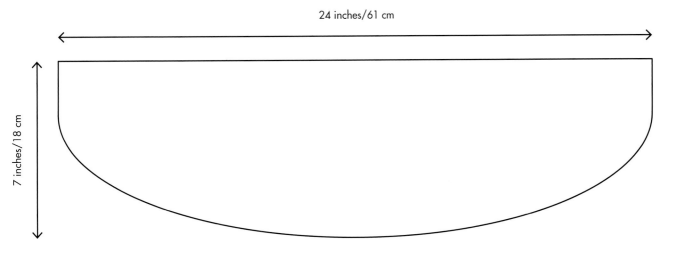

NOT TO SCALE: PRINT AT 125%

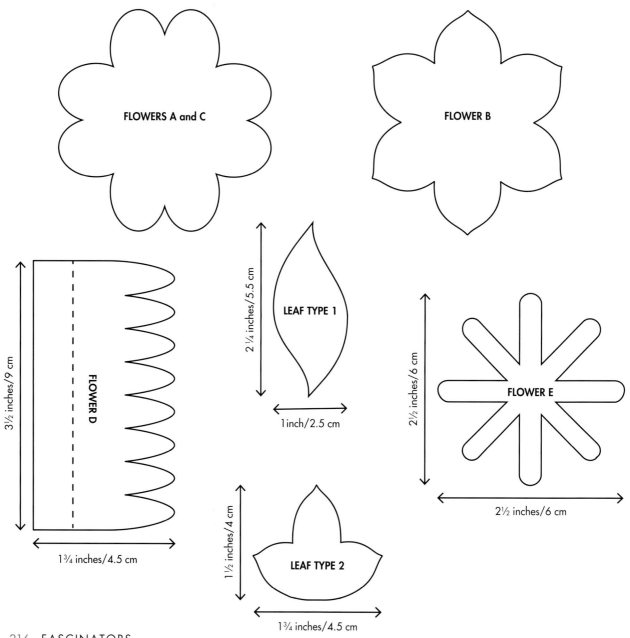

FLOWERS A and C

FLOWER B

LEAF TYPE 1

2 ¼ inches/5.5 cm

1 inch/2.5 cm

FLOWER D

3½ inches/9 cm

1¾ inches/4.5 cm

FLOWER E

2½ inches/6 cm

2½ inches/6 cm

LEAF TYPE 2

1½ inches/4 cm

1¾ inches/4.5 cm

ACKNOWLEDGMENTS

Many thanks to all those involved in making this book a success, in particular my wonderful mother, Julia, who inspired me to "create" from an early age and taught me much of what I know and now have the pleasure of passing onto others. An enormous amount of gratitude also to Ricky Baillie for the fabulous photography, as well as Colette, Hannah, Lyn, and Sakina for sorting out hair and makeup. And to all the beautiful models, including my gorgeous daughter, Nola.

Thanks to the editors and designers for their advice and hard work. Finally, a huge thank you to my eternally patient, positive, and supportive husband, Daniel, without whom I couldn't do any of this.

CREDITS

All fascinators by Hannah Scheidig (www.hannahsmillinery.com, www.arabellabridal.com, and www.madebycraftparties.com)

Photography: Step-by-step guide photography and photos for projects 24 and 25 by Hannah Scheidig, and all other photography by Ricky Baillie Photography (www.rickybaillie.com)

Hair by Sakina Sher and Hannah Scott

Makeup by Lyn Mckenzie (www.lynmckenziemakeup.co.uk) and Colette Casher Make-Up Artistry (www.colettecasher.com)

Models: Julie M, Maggie, and Maya (Superior Model Management), Emily Jones, Tessa Crolla, Lia Baillie, Corinna L. Benson, and Nola Scheidig

INDEX

Page numbers in *italics* indicate photographs of the finished fascinator.

adhesives, 17
Amanda, 70–74, *70*, *74*
Amelia, 99–105, *100*, *105*, 214
Anna, 178–184, *179*, *184*

barrettes, 17
basic sewing tools, 18
beads, 15
Bethany, 86–92, *87*, *92*
blanket stitch, 18–20
bridal fascinators
    about, 185
    Carly, 192–196, *193*, *196*
    Vivienne, 186–191, *187*, *191*
burning feathers, 40–43

Cara, *136*, 137–142, *142*
Carly, 192–196, *193*, *196*
children's fascinators
    about, 197
    Lola, 204–211, *205*, *211*
    Milly, 198–203, *199*, *203*
combs, 16

crin, 14
crocodile hair clips, 17
curling feathers, 36–39

difficult projects
    Cara, *136*, 137–142, *142*
    Emily, 131–136, *132*, *136*
    Sadie, 124–130, *125*, *130*

easy projects
    Amanda, 70–74, *70*, *74*
    Carly, 192–196, *193*, *196*
    Lia, 75–79, *76*, *79*
    Mariella, 54–59, *55*, *59*
    Mia, 150–155, *151*, *155*
    Milly, 198–203, *199*, *203*
    Naomi, 65–69, *66*, *69*
    Olivia, 156–162, *157*, *162*
    Ottilie, 80–85, *81*, *85*
    Summer, 145–149, *146*, *149*
    Vivienne, 186–191, *187*, *191*
    Zara, 60–64, *61*, *64*
elastic, hat, 16
Eloise, 112–116, *113*, *116*
Emily, 131–136, *132*, *136*

fabric, 15
fabric flowers
    making, 44–51
    as material, 17
Fabri-Tac glue, 17
feathers
    burning, 40–43
    curling, 36–39
    as material, 15
floral crowns
    about, 143–144
    Isla, 163–169, *164*, *169*
    Mia, 150–155, *151*, *155*
    Olivia, 156–162, *157*, *162*
    Summer, 145–149, *146*, *149*
flower-making tool kit, 17
flowers
    making fabric, 44–51
    silk or fabric, 17
    tool kit for, 17

glue, 17
grosgrain ribbon, 15

hair clips, 17
hairbands, 16
hat block, 15, 30
hat elastic, 16
headbands, 16
horsehair, 14

hot glue gun, 17

intermediate projects
    Amelia, 99–105, *100*, *105*, 214
    Anna, 178–184, *179*, *184*
    Bethany, 86–92, *87*, *92*
    Eloise, 112–116, *113*, *116*
    Isabella, 171–177, *172*, *177*
    Isla, 163–169, *164*, *169*
    Jasmine, 117–123, *118*, *123*, 215
    Lola, 204–211, *205*, *211*
    Thea, 106–111, *107*, *111*
    Tia, 93–98, *94*, *98*
Isabella, 171–177, *172*, *177*
Isla, 163–169, *164*, *169*

Jasmine, 117–123, *118*, *123*, 215

lace, 14
Lia, 75–79, *76*, *79*
Lola, 204–211, *205*, *211*, 216

mannequin head, 17
Mariella, 54–59, *55*, *59*
materials, 14–17
Mia, 150–155, *151*, *155*
Milly, 198–203, *199*, *203*

Naomi, 65–69, *66*, *69*
netting, 14

Olivia, 156–162, *157*, *162*
Ottilie, 80–85, *81*, *85*

Petersham ribbon, 15
pillbox hat base, 30–32

ribbon
    grosgrain, 15
    Petersham, 15
running stitch, 18

Sadie, 124–130, *125*, *130*
sewing tools, 18
silk flowers, 17
sinamay
    making base from, 25–29
    making bias strips from, 21–24
    as material, 14
    rolling sinamay edge, 33–35
stab stitch, 18–19
stiffener, 15
stitches, 18–20
straight stitch, 18
Summer, 145–149, *146*, *149*

techniques
    burning feathers, 40–43
    curling feathers, 36–39
    making a sinamay base, 25–29
    making fabric flowers, 44–51
    making sinamay bias strips, 21–24
    pillbox hat base, 30–32
    rolling sinamay edge, 33–35
    stitches, 18–20
templates
    Amelia, 214
    birdcage veil, 213
    Jasmine, 215
    Lola, 216
    rose petals, 212
Thea, 106–111, *107*, *111*
Tia, 93–98, *94*, *98*
tiaras
    about, 170
    Anna, 178–184, *179*, *184*
    Isabella, 171–177, *172*, *177*
tools, 17–18

veiling, 14
Vivienne, 186–191, *187*, *191*

wire, 17

Zara, 60–64, *61*, *64*

Notes

Notes